MW01273482

The Wealthy English Teacher: Teach, Travel, and Secure Your Financial Future

Jackie Bolen

Copyright 2015 by Jackie Bolen

All rights reserved. No part of this publication may be reproduced, distributed, or transmitted in any form or by any means, including photocopying, recording or other electronic or mechanical means without the prior written permission of the publisher, except in the case of brief quotations in critical reviews and certain other noncommercial uses permitted by copyright law. For permission requests, write to the publisher/author at the address below.

Jackie Bolen: jb.business.online@gmail.com
Visit the author at: www.jackiebolen.com

Table of Contents

Preface..5

Who Am I?..6

The Two-Fold Strategy: Increase Income and Decrease Expenses....................7

Step 1: Choose Your Job Wisely..8

  Salary, Legal Overtime Opportunities and Visas......................................8

  Airfare and Housing..11

  Taxes and Healthcare..11

  Where to Teach: "Good" Countries...12

  Where to Teach: "Okay" Countries...14

  Where to Teach: "Bad" Countries..16

Step 2: Build a Small Emergency Fund..17

Step 3: Live Frugally and Pay off Debts..18

  The Power of Compound Interest..18

  The Debt Snowball...20

  Top 10 Frugal Living Tips...22

    Tip #1: Choose your Friends Wisely...22

    Tip #2: Transportation...22

    Tip #3: Eating and Food...24

    Tip #4: Travel and Vacation..25

    Tip #5: Drinking..25

    Tip #6: Choose Your Hobbies Wisely..26

    Tip #7: Cost of Living AKA Bills...27

    Tip #8: Plan your Day...28

    Tip #9: Clothes and Shopping..28

    Tip #10: What is the Cheapest Option?...29

  Is It Ever Too Late to Start?...29

Step 4: Advance Your Career..31

Step 5: Build a Full Emergency Fund...34

A Special Note for Readers New to Investing...35

Step 6: Save $5,000 and Research Investment Options.................................36

  Do your Research 36

  Why You Need at Least $5,000 to Get Started.......................................37

  Brokerage Options for Expats...38

    Brokerage Options for Non-Americans...38

    Brokerage Options for Americans...39

  Mutual Funds, ETFs, Bonds and Individual Stocks..................................40

  Why Mutual Funds are Terrible..40

  Stock and Bond ETFs: Excellent Alternatives to Mutual Funds...................42

  Dividend Paying Stocks: also a Good Alternative to Mutual Funds...............48

    Five Basic Principles of Dividend Stock Investing..............................49

    How to Choose Which Stocks to Buy...51

    The Key Metrics I Look at..53

  What I Hold in My Portfolio: Stocks and ETFs.......................................55

  Trading vs. Investing..56

I'm Scared of the Stock Market! 58
What about Gold and Silver? 59
What about Pension Schemes? 61
Maybe I will Just Depend on the Government in Retirement 61
Step 7: Invest in the Financial Markets and Enjoy Life 63
How to Buy a Stock or ETF 63
What Next? Collect Dividends and Keep Investing 66
When to Sell a Stock or ETF 67
Investing on the Margin 69
Speculative Stocks and ETFs 70
Futures Contracts, and Shorting Stocks 71
Enjoy Life a Bit 72
The Cost per Use Model 73
Budget Travel Tips 74
Step 8: Build Passive Income Streams 77
HubPages 77
Affiliate Programs 78
Amazon 79
Iherb 79
Agoda 80
Writing E-books 80
Top 5 Tips for Self-Publishing an E-Book 81
Step 9: Plan for the Future--Working and Insurance 83
Working 83
Is Insurance Necessary? 84
Supplementary Health Insurance 84
Life Insurance 85
Step 10: Enjoy Financial Freedom 86
Before You Go 88
Resources: Tax Information for Expats 89
Canadians 89
Americans 91
Non North-Americans 92
Australia 92
New Zealand 92
The UK 92
Resources: Books, Websites and Podcasts 94
Books 94
Websites: Investing 101 for Beginners 94
Websites: Investing 95
Websites: Brokerages 95
Websites: Teaching Jobs 96
Websites: Passive Income 96
Financial Calculators 97
Podcasts: Investing 97
Podcasts: Passive Income Building 97

Preface

This book is for anyone looking to secure their financial future and more specifically, teachers living and working overseas, or those finishing university and considering teaching abroad as a career. Freedom from worrying about money is an achievable goal for just about anyone by following some simple steps. However, this journey is not for the faint of heart. It will require a good dose of dedication, sacrifice and frugal living especially in the early years and you will have to live in a way that is different from those around you. It is however, well worth it when you are not a slave to debt because you will have so many more choices: working, or not; taking a job not based entirely on salary; semi-retiring to some beautiful place in your forties or fifties; taking time off of work to travel or volunteer. All these things really are possible, even for someone who chooses to teach abroad for their career. This book will cover the ten steps to financial freedom including:

1. Choosing a job wisely (with advice most specifically tailored to ESL Teachers)
2. Building a small emergency fund
3. Living frugally and paying off debts
4. Advancing your career
5. Building a full emergency fund
6. Saving your first $5,000 to invest
7. Investing in the financial markets and enjoying life
8. Building passive income streams
9. Planning for the future
10. Enjoying financial freedom

Before we get too deep into the world of money and finance, I would like to give a big thanks to my editor, Jason Ryan. Nothing gets by him! I really appreciated his help in making this book as awesome as it could be.

A note about the currencies in this book. They are all United States Dollars (USD), unless otherwise noted.

Who Am I?

You may be wondering who I am and why you should be taking my advice about achieving financial freedom. I will start off by saying that I am just a regular kind of person with no formal training in career development or personal finance but that I have been actively researching and writing about these topics for the past ten years (see my blog: *My Life! Teaching in a Korean University- www.teachinginkoreanuniversity.com*).

Even when I was a kid, I was interested in financial stuff and I remember reading just about any finance or investing magazine or book that I could get my hands on; I bought my first mutual funds when I was still in high school from money that I had saved up from my part-time job at McDonald's. I have also helped numerous friends get started and stay motivated on the path towards financial success in their own lives. I am no financial guru, but this is far from a weakness because it means that I understand where the average person is coming from. I guarantee a book free of jargon and complicated things that the average sixth grader would find difficult to comprehend. It really is a book for just about everyone, even the total beginner just getting started with planning out their financial future.

I am originally from Canada but have been living in South Korea for the past ten years and teaching at universities for the last eight. I have transformed myself during that time from an average kind of twenty-two year old just out of university with student loans to totally debt-free and about $200,000 US in investments and multiple passive income streams bringing in around $1000 US per month. I now travel the world, taking two exotic vacations a year and generally just enjoy my life, although I still live frugally most of the time. Once you get started with frugal living, it is pretty hard to stop! My long-term goal for the future is to become a financial advisor and help others in a more formal kind of way as well as continue down the path towards further financial freedom in my own life. I plan to return to Canada in the next year or two and go back to school so I can achieve this goal.

You can find me on various places around the web, but the best place to start is *www.jackiebolen.com*. This site has links to everything else as well as information on how to connect with me on social media. Feel free to contact me at jb.business.online@gmail.com.

The Two-Fold Strategy: Increase Income and Decrease Expenses

The premise of this book is that financial freedom depends on two factors: increasing income and decreasing expenses and making sure that income ALWAYS exceeds expenses each month for the rest of your life, except for some extenuating circumstance. It is almost deceptively simple, but it is something that many people fail to remember when they are just living their lives not thinking consciously about it. There are many people who consistently spend more money than they have coming in each month, living beyond their means, financing this lifestyle with things like credit cards or lines of credit. That is to say nothing about emergencies: a car breaks down, a child gets sick, someone loses a job but with some careful planning and preparation these things do not need to mean financial ruin and although they might be annoying, they do not need to be cause for despair.

Essentially, people get into serious financial trouble because their expenses exceed their income. Conversely, people achieve financial success when their income exceeds their expenses and they put this extra money to use wisely. Teachers have a rather limited range of salaries so although it is indeed possible to increase your salary (see Step 1: Choose Your Job Wisely and Step 8: Build Passive Income Streams), most of us will have to focus attention on decreasing our expenses (see Step 3: Live Frugally and Pay Off Debts). Let's now turn our attention to the first step in securing your financial future: choosing a job wisely.

Step 1: Choose Your Job Wisely

This section will contain advice most applicable to ESL (English as a Second Language)/EFL (English as a Foreign Language) teachers but could be helpful to international school teachers as well. It will contain two parts: general things to consider and then "good," "okay," and "bad" countries to teach English in (in terms of employment packages).

When you are looking to teach abroad, there are a variety of factors to consider beyond just the basic salary including legal overtime opportunities, whether or not you own your working visa, airfare, housing, taxes, healthcare, number of teaching hours, sick days, and vacation.

For example, *Job A* might have the highest salary of any other offers, but you could be stuck at school for 50 hours per week, with 30-35 teaching hours, which will leave you exhausted and burnt out in short order. *Job B* might have one of the lowest salaries, but it has a low number of working hours as well as lots of vacation. If there are plenty of legal overtime opportunities, it could actually be a better deal than *Job A*. Or, *Job C* might have a low salary and a high amount of teaching hours, but it could be an excellent move for your career and a company in which you can advance in, in which case you should consider turning down a higher salary or low teaching hours job that has no room for growth or advancement. The decision is a complicated one and is not something that should be taken lightly. I will talk briefly about the various factors to consider.

Salary, Legal Overtime Opportunities and Visas

Salary will (and should) be a major factor when deciding on a job offer, especially if you have significant amounts of debt to pay off or want to kick-start your journey to financial freedom. However, I would like to suggest a more helpful way of examining it than just simply going for the highest number possible. A better variable to consider is salary per hour worked. By having a job with the highest salary per hour worked possible, you will have one of two things: a lot of money coming in each month or plenty of free time on your hands to pursue other things such as overtime opportunities, building passive income streams or advancing your career in some way.

I will give you three examples from South Korea, which is the context that I am most familiar with. Let's assume for the sake of simplicity that housing or adequate housing allowance is included in all cases (as is usually the case in South Korea). Also, to keep things from getting overly complicated, I will not factor in healthcare or taxes, which are the same for all jobs. As a quick reference, 1,000 South Korean Won is generally equivalent to around $1 USD, so 2.4 million Korean Won is around $2,400 USD.

The Average Hagwon (Private Institute) Job

Monthly salary: 2.4 million Korean Won

Weekly teaching hours: 30

Vacation: 2 weeks/year

Airfare: included (2 million Won)

Bonus money at end of contract: 2.4 million Won

Total yearly salary: 33.2 million Won

Total hours worked/year: 1500

Salary/hour = 22,000 Won

The Average University Job

Monthly salary: 2.2 million Korean Won

Weekly teaching hours: 15

Vacation: 20 weeks/year

Airfare: not included

Bonus money at end of contract: not included

Total yearly salary: 26.4 million Won

Total hours worked/ year: 480

Salary/hour = 55,000 Won

The Average Public School Job

Monthly salary: 2.0 million Korean won

Weekly teaching hours: 22

Vacation: 14 days (officially), but there are many "desk-warming" days where you have to be at school but have no classes or work that you need to do. I will include some of these, so vacation is around 6 weeks (unofficially), which is what I will use for my calculations.

Airfare: included (2 million Won)

Bonus money at end of contract: 2.0 million Won

Total yearly salary: 28 million Won

Total hours worked: 1012

Salary/hour = 28,000 Won

As you can see from these three examples, the hagwon job which at first glance seems like the best one due to the high monthly salary, free airfare and contract completion bonus is the worst one in terms of salary per hour due to the high number of teaching hours and low vacation time. The public school job that initially seems to be the worst due to the low monthly salary turns out to be better than the hagwon job because it pays 6000 Won more per teaching hour. And of course, the university job is by far the best, but these jobs are not that easy to come by in South Korea and require some serious qualifications and networking skills (for tips on how to get one of these coveted jobs, check out this book, available on *Amazon* in both Kindle and print editions: *How to Get a University Job in South Korea*).

Another closely related factor to consider when deciding on a job offer is the availability of *legal* overtime opportunities. There is always plenty of *illegal* work you could do on the side but I do not recommend this, especially if you are someone like me who likes to stay on the right side of the law. The best way to do legal overtime work is through your main place of employment. For example, some universities in Korea have a low number of teaching hours per week and large amounts of vacation. If you can combine this with lots of opportunities for work during those off times, you can make a significant amount of money and in some cases even double your monthly salary. Another way to work legal overtime is by working at a place that gives you permission for outside work and will sign whatever paperwork necessary to make it possible for you to do this, assuming it is permissible with immigration. Overtime opportunities should be something that you inquire about during the interview process.

Alternatively, you could work in a country where you own your own visa, such as Japan (as opposed to it being tied to a certain workplace like in Korea) and you will be free to accept as many jobs as you wish. It is beyond the scope of this book to give you a comprehensive list of which countries you hold your own visa in, but it is information that is readily found online with a bit of research on the specific countries that you are considering. Owning your work visa is also quite beneficial because you can leave a bad employer with minimal fuss, which is not the case in a place like Korea where visas are sponsored by your employer who you must *ask* to give you a letter of release and permission to leave and get a different job; immigration is also generally reluctant to get involved in employee--employer disputes, even in cases of breach of contract.

Airfare and Housing

Years ago, South Korea used to be quite a popular choice for English teachers due to the prepaid airfare and free housing offered in the employment package. These days, those kinds of offers are becoming more of a rarity, especially the prepaid airfare as the market is becoming more and more saturated with well-qualified teachers looking for work. While these things can save you money and hassle, I would suggest that they perhaps are not the most important factors to consider when choosing your job. Airfare can be found almost anywhere in the world for less than a thousand dollars and so it should not be a deciding factor even though it can be a nice bonus. If housing is not offered, there should be a higher monthly salary or housing allowance included in the contract. If not, look elsewhere; if a school is cheap in this aspect they are probably cheap in lots of other things as well (including paying you your salary in full and on time each month).

Taxes and Healthcare

Many countries where you might want to teach English have a very low tax rate (around 3-4% in South Korea for example) and excellent healthcare, which might be better than your home country, especially if you are from the USA. But, not all places are so favorable and in some countries like Vietnam, you may get 20% or more of your salary taken from you in taxes and healthcare costs. Like airfare and housing, taxes and healthcare should not be the biggest factors in making your decision about where to teach, but they should be considered especially when comparing otherwise similar job offers from different countries.

Where to Teach: "Good" Countries

In this section about good, okay and bad countries to teach in, I am making no judgements about a country's people or culture but am simply talking about the total employment package and working conditions for English teachers.

South Korea

Ten years ago, South Korea was one of the best places in the world to teach English due to the high salary, extremely favourable exchange rate with the USA and Canada, free housing and airfare along with minimal qualifications and low expectations for teachers. These days, cost of living has risen significantly while salaries have stagnated and qualifications and expectations for teachers have risen so that it is not the prime location it once was. However, there is definitely money to be made and saved, especially if you are willing to live frugally. Most teachers can put away around $1,000 per month with little effort and live quite well. For others, with some effort and frugal living, they can save up to $1,500 per month (and more if they are doing overtime or have permission from their visa sponsor to teach at other companies or schools). Another way to live well in Korea is by working your way up the job ladder into a university, which has a very low number of working hours and lots of vacation. If you do some overtime work during those down times, you can increase your savings potential significantly, up to $4,000-5,000 per month.

The Middle East

The Middle East, especially Saudi Arabia, is filled with jobs that have extremely high salaries and other bonuses such as tax-free salary, free airfare, housing and healthcare (look on the International job board at *ESL Cafe* and you will notice that a large number of the jobs there are from Saudi). It is really possible for the average English teacher to save at least

$2,000 per month and some people can save significantly more than that. The down-side is that qualifications are quite high and often require a related degree of some sort (Education, English, or TESOL) and a CELTA (usually a 1 month program) or TEFL certification (120 hour course minimum, with an in-class component) even for the entry-level jobs. The top jobs usually require a related master's degree and several years of experience.

The biggest down-side is the culture, especially for women and LGBT people, where it can sometimes be dangerous. For people who are used to living in western countries, or in places like Korea or Japan it can be extremely difficult to adapt to things like not being able to drive, drink alcohol freely in public, leave the house by yourself, wearing a head covering and living on a compound. In addition, if you are single, you will probably find that your dating opportunities are extremely limited. But, if you can manage it for two or three years, it can provide an extremely solid foundation for your financial future. Three years in Saudi in exchange for $100,000 in the bank at the end is worth it for some people.

Vietnam

Vietnam is an up and coming English teaching destination and where many of the teachers from Japan and Korea are ending up as they look for greener pastures. The economy is booming and they offer a good combination of decent salaries (around $20 per hour), low cost of living, relaxed culture (especially after somewhere like the Middle East or Korea), and amazing food and travel opportunities. They have all the big companies like International House and the British Council, which if you can get a job at, is a good step towards advancing your career into management or teacher-training and they also have a massive number of international schools, which are an excellent choice if you are a certified teacher. If I were to continue in my career as a teacher after Korea, Vietnam would be my number one choice. The biggest downside is the tax rate of around 15-20%, which is higher than most other places popular with English teachers.

Malaysia

Along with Vietnam, Malaysia is a place that you will find lots of teachers who used to teach in Korea or Japan but have moved onto bigger and better things. While there are not that many English teaching jobs in Malaysia, the ones that are available are excellent in terms of salary, professionalism and vacation--especially the mentor-teacher ones where you travel

13

to public schools and work with the local English teachers.

Hong Kong

Jobs are not that easy to find in Hong Kong, and seem to be filled mostly by PhD holders, or people certified to teach in public schools in their home country. The jobs available to those with only bachelor's degrees seem to be generally limited to kindergartens which can involve long hours. However, if you are lucky enough to get a job in Hong Kong, you will likely enjoy it because the salaries are high and teachers are treated like professionals. There is plenty of Western influence in Hong Kong and thousands of Western expats so that you can buy anything you want, do any activity that you can think of, or get service in English.

Where to Teach: "Okay" Countries

Japan

Japan is very similar to Korea in terms of salary and total employment package except it has a few things which are not ideal when compared to Korea, which is why it gets placed into the "okay" category instead of the "good" category. One very positive thing about Japan is that you own your own visa which means that you are free to move around from job to job with minimal hassle; this can eliminate much of the shady behaviour of employers in places like Korea or China where employers hold much more power over employees. However, on the downside you will most often have to pay for your own airfare and housing and the cost of living is extremely high, especially for eating, drinking and transportation. In Korea, teachers can go out for a night on the town five days a week and still not burn through their entire salary, whereas in Japan doing this even once a week will significantly cut into your savings potential. If you live frugally in Japan, it is possible to save around $1,000 per month but you will have to be much more disciplined about it than you would in Korea, Vietnam, Malaysia, Hong Kong, the Middle East or just about any other country in the world. In addition, university jobs in Japan are much more difficult to obtain than compared to Korea or the Middle East.

China

China is very similar to Vietnam in that it is an up and coming country with a growing economy and rising salaries for ESL teachers but has a very low cost of living, especially outside Beijing and Shanghai. It also has the huge advantage of having an in-demand language that could benefit you greatly in your future career if you use your time there to become fluent. China is not in the top-rated group for a few reasons including: while salaries for the private institute jobs are reasonably high (but you will have to work hard for it--around 30 teaching hours/week), they are very low for university jobs, and it is quite difficult to find a quality job in China simply because it is such a big place and there is not that much information.

Perhaps the biggest drawbacks and the main reasons why I would not go there are the pollution and lack of safety standards for things like food, manufactured items and infrastructure, police unwillingness to get involved in any disputes involving a foreigner, difficulty in getting money out of the country, a very poor quality of health care as well as lack of freedom as it relates to the Internet. I depend on things like *Facebook* to keep me connected with my friends and family around the world and do not want to have to deal with trying to get around this with proxy servers and other such annoying things.

Russia

I have a couple of friends who made the move from Korea to Russia and have been very happy with it. They have made many good friends there and have only positive things to say about their places of employment and how professional it is. Salaries are decent and the cost of living is not too expensive so it is possible to save a decent amount of money each month. If you are white, you have the additional bonus of blending in with the locals and not being a target for things like crime or weird people on the street or subway like you are in some of the Asian or Middle Eastern countries. The main drawback would be the weather. I left Canada because it was just too cold for me and I was not happy spending most of winter indoors so moving somewhere like Russia would not be ideal for me.

Taiwan

Many people think that Taiwan is quite similar to Japan, Korea or China but it is actually more similar to a South-East Asian country in terms of lifestyle, people, food and weather. Many English teachers end up staying for a long time and really enjoy their lives there. Money-saving potential is good but you will be expected to work pretty hard for your money with average salaries around $15-$20 per hour and with things like housing or airfare not included in salary packages. But on the upside, cost of living is cheaper than in places like Japan or Korea. If you stay for a few years you can make connections through networking and work your way up into better jobs, as you would in any country. If salaries were slightly higher (in the $25-30 per hour range) it would be one of the best choices for English teachers in the world.

Where to Teach: "Bad" Countries

South-East Asia and South/Central America

With the exception of Malaysia, Vietnam (see "good" countries) and Singapore (very few jobs there), I would consider South-East Asia including Myanmar, Laos, Cambodia, Thailand, and Indonesia, as well as South and Central America bad job locations simply because the salaries are so low and infrastructure including things like transportation and Internet speeds might be lacking especially in places like Cambodia or Myanmar. If you do decide to teach in any of these places, you will probably have the best year or two of your entire life, but you will find it very hard to save a significant amount of money. If I had to make a guess, in terms of money-saving potential, five or six years in Thailand would probably equal one year in Korea or six months in the Middle East. On the upside, if you do teach in Central or South America, you will have the advantage of getting a chance to learn a "useful" language that can benefit you in your future career, especially if you are American.

Europe

Europe is a big place, so for the sake of this discussion, I will divide it into Eastern Europe (Romania, Czech Republic, Slovakia, etc.) and Western Europe (France, Spain, Italy, etc.). I have no doubt that if you teach in Europe, similar to South-East Asia it will be the best year or two of your life. Delicious beer and wine, amazing food, friendly people and a lifestyle that feels kind of like your home-country. While Eastern Europe does have a reasonably low cost of living, it does have one distinct disadvantage in that salaries for ESL teachers are very low due to huge numbers of qualified people looking for jobs. Cities like Prague turn out massive amounts of CELTA and DELTA qualified teachers so competition for jobs can be fierce and I would classify it as an employer's market. In Western Europe, salaries for ESL

16

teachers are slightly higher but the cost of living is very high, and most teachers will find it a struggle to save a significant amount of money each month.

Step 2: Build a Small Emergency Fund

Now that you have made a wise decision about where to teach and have gotten settled there, it is time to build a small emergency fund. Ideally, you would have done this before you moved because it is always good to have a plane ticket and a couple months' expenses socked away in case things go bad with your new country or place of employment. However, if you do not have this, it is time to save up your first $2,000, which you will hopefully be able to do within the first two or three months of teaching abroad. I chose $2,000 because for $1,000, you should be able to get a plane ticket home or to another destination and then you will have another $1,000 to tide you over until you find work of some sort. I recommend keeping the money in a place that is easily accessible and by easily accessible, I mean available immediately in case of emergency, preferably in a separate bank account in your adopted country. Keeping it in your home country, but easily accessible with a debit or credit card is a good option too. Do not worry about earning lots of interest on this money because that is not its purpose.

You should maintain this small emergency fund at all times until you have reached Step 5 where you will build your full emergency fund and if you must dip into it for some reason, replace it as soon as possible and by as soon as possible, I mean your next paycheck. Reasons to dip into it would include emergency medical or dental care, or needing to go back home in case of a family member's serious illness or death. This does not include things like: going on vacation, buying food, drinks, and home furnishings, replacing a broken computer or cell-phone, and everyday medical and dental expenses for yourself or your pets.

Step 3: Live Frugally and Pay off Debts

After you have built up your small emergency fund of $2,000, it is time to turn all your attention towards paying off debt, including credit cards and student loans. If you do not have any debt, count your lucky stars and congratulate yourself on your good sense (or financial support from your family during your university years) and skip directly to Step 4: Advance Your Career and Step 5: Build a Full Emergency Fund. However, if you are like most people heading overseas to teach for the first time, you will have student loans and perhaps some other types of debt like a car loan, credit cards, or health expenses. The key to getting your financial future off to a healthy start is by paying off these debts *as quickly as possible* because of the power of compound interest.

The Power of Compound Interest

Albert Einstein is rumored to have said that compound interest is the most powerful force in the universe. While people are not sure whether or not he actually said that, it is indeed a very powerful thing and it is something that can either make you rich or poor. *The key is to have compound interest work for you* (through savings and investments) *and not against you* (through credit cards, student loans or other debt).

Investopedia defines **compound interest** as:

> "Interest calculated on the initial principal and also on the accumulated interest of previous periods of a deposit or loan. Compound interest can be thought of as "interest on interest," and will make a deposit or loan grow at a faster rate than simple interest, which is interest calculated only on the principal amount. The rate at which compound interest accrues depends on the frequency of compounding; the higher the number of compounding periods, the greater the compound interest. Thus, the amount of compound interest accrued on $100 compounded at 10% annually will be lower than that on $100 compounded at 5% semi-annually over the same time period. Compound interest is also known as compounding."

Compound Interest Works for You

For example, let's take $1,000 US, which is what you might get in gifts from your parents and other relatives for a graduation present when you are around 22 years of age and finishing university. You wisely decide to put this money into a high interest account instead of spending it on junk. Let's see how much this money will be worth by the time you retire by using a compound interest calculator (search online for one). That $1,000 will grow to $3,565 by the time you are 65, assuming a very modest interest rate of 3%. Even better is if you can add money to your account each month--maybe $100, which should not be much of a stretch for most people. By the time you are 65, you would have an astounding $109,000 and for very little work, thanks to the power of compound interest. The way compound interest works is that the longer the time it has to work its magic, the better off you will be because you earn interest on the interest as well as the principal (**principal** = the amount of money you deposit) and on it goes. Start early by paying off your debts as quickly as possible and investing as much as possible in your twenties and thirties and you will set yourself up for a very bright financial future. If you wait until your forties or fifties to begin investing it will be an uphill battle because you have so few years for the compounding magic to happen.

Compound Interest Works Against You

Conversely, compound interest can work against you. Let's take an example of a typical vacation of $2,000 which you decided to reward yourself with upon finishing university. This vacation is financed entirely on credit cards and paid off over a long period of time, mostly just by meeting the minimum monthly payments. Assuming an annual interest rate of 17% (normal for credit cards!) and payments of $50 per month, that two week vacation will take you 60 months, or five years to pay off. Your dream vacation will cost you around $3,000 and not the $2,000 that you thought it would. Was it worth it? Probably not. Check out a credit card (or student loan) payment calculator to make your own calculations.

Let's do one more example using student loans, which is perhaps a more typical scenario than graduation gifts or credit card debt for someone just out of college and considering their first teaching job overseas. Let's assume $50,000 in loans, with an interest rate of 5%. Paid off over four years teaching English abroad, you would end up paying around $56,400 ($50,000 principal + $6,4000 interest), but paid off over 20 years, it would cost you $79,200 ($50,000 principal + $29,200 interest). Scary stuff, right? Clearly, it is extremely beneficial for your financial future to pay off debt as quickly as possible. There are various methods and plans for doing this, but the one that I recommend is Dave Ramsey's debt snowball.

Calculations can have different results depending on which calculator you use because when and how the interest is calculated varies. However, this is not so important and the main point is that you should always *pay off your debts as quickly as possible* to reduce the amount of interest paid.

The Debt Snowball

For more details about paying off debts as quickly as possible, I highly recommend checking out Dave Ramsey's book, *The Total Money Makeover.* He also has a daily podcast/radio show (check the iT*unes* store), and is active on social media such as *Twitter.* I can give you the basics here which may be enough to get you started on the process. The first thing you need to do is figure out how much all your debts are and list them on a single piece of paper from the smallest to largest. For some disorganized people, this may be a bigger task than it actually sounds like, but do not get discouraged because it is vital to know what you are dealing with; an accurate picture of your debts is absolutely necessary for planning your attack.

A quick note about debt . . . you can divide it into two separate categories: debt related to a physical object of some sort that you can sell like a car and debt related to a non-physical thing or something that you cannot sell like student loans or medical expenses. If you have debt related to an object, I recommend you sell it, **immediately** and preferably before you ever left your home country, especially if it is a car. If you decide to return home, you could buy yourself a cheap used car within a few hours of getting off the plane, so it is really unnecessary to keep throwing money into a depreciating asset (one that goes down in value) while you are overseas.

Once you have this list, get into attack mode and go after the smallest debt first, paying minimum payments on all other debts and hitting this one with all the extra money that you possibly can. In order to get this extra money you need to be working nights and weekends, doing whatever you can to make a bit of extra money. You also need to live very frugally, eating beans and rice, rice and beans (I would mix in a few veggies for health reasons!) as Dave Ramsey likes to say for as long as it takes to pay off your debt. When you pay off the smallest debt, move on to the next smallest one and attack it, while continuing to pay minimum payments on all the other debt. You will keep freeing up more and more money as you pay off the smaller debts and then you can attack the bigger debts even more quickly. The snowball picks up speed and starts rolling faster as time goes on.

One area where I disagree slightly with Dave Ramsey is how he does not differentiate between loans with low and high interest rates. His thinking is that the psychological benefits of paying off debts quickly outweigh the possible money-saving advantage of paying off the high interest ones first. While a loan with a 6% interest rate and one with an 8% rate are basically the same and you should follow Dave Ramsey's plan, a student loan with a rate of 3% and a credit card with a 20% rate are not and clearly the credit card should be paid off first. You will have to use your discretion; a good rule of thumb is to pay off the smallest ones first if the interest rates are within 5% of each other. If you pay off something in a year or two, an interest rate difference of a few percent is not really that important. However, if the difference is greater than 5%, pay off the ones with the highest interest rates first.

A quick note about credit cards. It is often possible to negotiate with credit card companies for a reduction in the interest rate on your debt. Be persistent and keep calling, asking to speak to the manager if the front-line person is not getting you the results you want. It is also sometimes possible to offer a lump-sum payment to close out your account that is far less than the actual debt amount, especially if you are behind on your minimum monthly payments. It does not hurt to ask. However, remember these two things: ALWAYS get the offer in writing and NEVER give a credit card company (or debt collection agency) electronic access to your bank account. There is a wealth of information about this topic; search on Google for something like, "Lump-Sum Payment Credit Card."

Dave Ramsey is a serious advocate of making a written budget, even if you have no debts. I tend to agree with him as putting everything on paper forces you to be disciplined and organized in your financial plan. Check out his book which has a section on the basics of budgeting, or one of hundreds of websites or apps (search for something like "sample budget") and find a system that works for you. For some people, using a smartphone app works well but for others, they prefer the "envelope" method. Besides budgeting, never forget that attack mode also requires frugal living. Here are my top ten frugal living tips geared specifically for expats living abroad.

Top 10 Frugal Living Tips

Tip #1: Choose your Friends Wisely

A common saying is that you are only as good (or bad) as the average of the five people that you spend the most time with. Intuitively, we know that the people around us can subtlety, or not so subtlety influence our thinking and spending decisions. When you are new to a place, it can be tempting to become fast friends with the first couple of people who show you a bit of kindness or a co-worker that you happen to have a bit of a connection with, but they may not actually be the best people for you to be around, especially if they have a lot of debt and are not worried about paying it off. Or, maybe they have already paid off their students loans and are now in "spend without regard" mode, in which case you will probably end up spending more money than you want hanging around them. Another group of people that may not be good for you are the ones who have a different kind of job such as an engineer or US military professionals who might make significantly more money than you. For them, a thirty dollar dinner or a fifty dollar bottle of wine might be nothing, but for you, it can seriously blow your budget.

The best kind of people that you could hang around with are the locals, or other teachers who make a similar amount of money to you and are focused on paying off their debts as well. The locals will have the best tips for how to live well, cheaply and will usually know the best value restaurants, shopping spots and local markets for groceries. Other expats who are in the same situation as you will appreciate social activities and time spent together that do not require large outlays of cash.

Tip #2: Transportation

While you are paying off your debts, I *strongly* recommend not having a car because there is no faster way to eat up large amounts of money. Once you pay off your debts and are in the 'enjoy life a bit' mode, a car could be a possibility for you. Related to this is using taxis.

While convenient and fast, they are also very expensive and a bad habit to get into, even in places like South Korea or Vietnam where they are reasonably cheap. If you do not want to walk or ride a bicycle, the subway or bus is a much better option than a car or taxi.

What I do recommend is walking, even if other people think it is really not possible to walk from point A to point B in your town, it often does not take as long as you might think. When I lived in Cheonan, South Korea and I was trying to pay off my grad school loans, I used to walk almost everywhere--to buy groceries, to hang out with friends on the other side of town, to the movie theater and and to go hiking on the mountains. It is excellent exercise and a great opportunity to think, or listen to some audio books or podcasts. It is an extremely frugal thing to do on two counts: free exercise and saving money on taxis, buses or subways. Of course, you should use a decent pair of running shoes to avoid any injuries.

Another form of frugal transportation is bicycling. You can cover much longer distances, faster by biking than by walking and it is possible to do it almost all year-round in most places if you dress for the weather. In my early years in South Korea, I bought an extremely cheap bike that fell apart within a few months after using it almost every day to ride to work. It was not one of my better financial choices and years later, I bought another, mid-range one that is much more comfortable and enjoyable to use and up to this point, I have ridden over 4,000km on it. I most often use it to exercise, but I also use it to go run errands in my neighborhood. Perhaps the best thing you can do when you get to a new place is find out where the foreign teachers "buy-sell-trade" things online and look for a decent used bike. People are disorganized and you can often find some excellent deals on things like bikes from people who are leaving the country in a few days and in a hurry to sell; you just need to be patient.

A quick safety note about bicycles (and scooters too). They can be very dangerous if you are in a new place and do not understand the rules of the road. I guarantee that almost anywhere will have a lot busier roads than in a place like Canada. Also, drivers will likely not behave the way you expect and traffic law enforcement may be low to non-existent. Always wear a helmet and do not ride with headphones in your ears. Try to stick to dedicated bike paths if possible. Make sure your health insurance coverage is adequate in case of an accident.

Tip #3: Eating and Food

Eating out is expensive, with the possible exception of some countries like Vietnam or Thailand where cheap and delicious street food is a viable option. In most countries, it will be significantly cheaper to cook and eat at home than to eat out. I recommend going "local" by eating the basics, things like fruit, vegetables, eggs, and rice or bread because you can get these things at the local supermarket and it will be significantly cheaper than trying to maintain a diet similar to your home country. Here in South Korea, you can get anything you could possibly imagine, imported by Costco or other companies, but you will pay an outrageous amount for it. For me, it is an occasional treat to frequent one of these places and not my everyday mode of operation.

Learning to cook is really easy and a skill that will be extremely beneficial in your life, both in terms of living frugally as well as for your health. If you do not know how to cook or shop for food on a budget, do not feel overwhelmed, but just start by learning a few basic things and perfecting three or four dishes. Search on *YouTube* for "How to make _____." You could start with some simple things like an omelet, French toast, tomato sauce and pasta, or vegetable soup. Or, make a local friend and ask them to teach you a few simple dishes. Failing that, *YouTube* can work some magic for you! Search for "Food + How to Cook/Make." Here in South Korea, things like kimchi chigae (kimchi stew), pajeon (green onion pancake) or kimchi bokumbap (kimchi fried rice) are extremely easy to make and you can find the ingredients very cheaply at local shops.

I will share a story to hopefully inspire you: I had one friend here in Korea who was obsessed with paying off a massive amount of student loans during his first year teaching abroad (around $30,000). He purposely took a job out in the countryside so as to not be tempted by the Western delights of the big city and he just watched downloaded movies, listened to downloaded music and read downloaded books for an entire year, living on a ridiculously small amount of money--something like $200 per month, including his Internet and other bills. For food, he bought a massive bag of rice and another bag of onions. He would supplement this with whatever fruit and vegetables were in season and really cheap. He used to get free lunch at school so he would eat a massive amount of it. During that year he paid off his entire loan and now, he is doing quite well for himself and has all sorts of investments, but it did take a year of sacrifice. You can do it too!

Tip #4: Travel and Vacation

Perhaps part of the reason you came overseas was to see a new part of the world and experience a different culture. However, if you have significant amounts of debt, you actually have no business jet-setting around the world and the best path for you to a debt free life and financial freedom in the future should be the "stay-cation." No matter how you spin it (couch-surfing, a great deal on a plane ticket, shared hostels, only street food), a vacation abroad is going to eat up significant amounts of money, which should be going towards your debt payments. A stay-cation really is not such a bad option, especially if you are new to a place. Explore your city, hang out with friends, or start a little project that you have been putting off. If you are serious about paying off debt, sacrifice is required and this is one area that is an obvious place to start. You can save at least $1,000 by staying home for a week instead of going abroad.

Tip #5: Drinking

I love a good expat bar. Nice import beers on tap, greasy bar food, staff that speak English, good music, trivia nights and all my friends can be found in one place. Who wouldn't love it? Except when I was paying off my debts and trying to save up my first $5,000 to invest in the stock market, I avoided them like the plague. They are dangerous for anyone trying to save money because before you know it, the night is over and you have spent $50 or more on food and drink and you might also have an expensive taxi ride home.

If you like to indulge in a drink or two, a far better plan for you is the "7-11 Bar" or the "Beach Bar" if you live in a coastal city like I do. In South Korea, convenience stores sell all sorts of local and imported beer and they usually have picnic tables or patio furniture set up outside the store where you can hang out and drink. Many other countries have similar sorts of arrangements and are not as worried about public drinking as North Americans are. A night out will cost you $10-20 instead of $50 or more.

Another option which I enjoy is to host a potluck at my house. I cook up a big pot of soup or something cheap like that, invite a few friends over and ask them to bring some food or drink. I will always have a few bottles of wine in my cupboard as well, which I get cheaply at the big supermarket (usually around $6-7 per bottle). We always have an enjoyable night and the best part is that I only have to take a few steps to my own bed at the end of the night.

Tip #6: Choose Your Hobbies Wisely

Just as choosing your friends wisely is important, you should also choose your hobbies very carefully. The best ones are free, or "free-ish." By "free-ish," I mean the ones like a board game or book club at a coffee shop where you are only expected to buy a cup of coffee, or a hiking club where the expense is just for transportation to and from the mountain, or a hobby that requires an Internet connection, which you already pay for every month. Some hobbies which I would recommend include:

Cooking It is healthy, frugal and fun once you get somewhat proficient at it; it is something that you can keep getting better at for the rest of your life. An idea that I have never done, but which I would love to do is to have a potluck club. Maybe every second Friday night, you and a few friends get together at a different house and share a meal and some drinks together.

Board Games Find some friends or a board game club in your town and enjoy playing games together. Some of my favorites are: King of Tokyo (beginner), Settlers of Catan or Small World (intermediate) and Puerto Rico or Pandemic (advanced). It can be a decent investment to get a couple games that you enjoy if you plan on playing them a lot. They are usually cheaper to buy in your home country than abroad so consider packing some in your suitcase with you. You could also compare some sites like *Amazon*, *Ebay* or *Cool Stuff Inc* with the local ones in the country where you are living.

Reading You can expand your mind while not opening up that wallet. Of course, you should not be buying your books online or at expensive bookstores. Instead, most towns with a decent number of expats have a book-swap or a take-one leave-one spot. If you can find a book club, it is even better because you can do some socializing in the process.

Exercise This topic has already been covered in the transportation section, but if you can walk or bike as your main form of moving from one place to the other, you will save a lot of money and get some exercise in the process. Otherwise, there are plenty of things you can do that do not involve spending money (avoid the gym--it can get expensive!) to stay healthy. Some of my favorite free exercises include videos at home (Yoga videos, or Jillian Michaels), running, hiking or swimming in the ocean in summer. Now that I have paid off my loans and have a significant amount of money invested, I have spent a bit of money on "splurges" and I now have a nice bicycle and stand up paddleboard that I use at least a few times a week in the warmer months. But, when you are paying off your debts, it is all about the free exercise.

Media By media, I mean things that you can get for free or cheap online with an Internet connection such as podcasts, movies, books, music, and TV shows.

Internet ventures I love writing and learning how to do new things on the Internet, so blogging and developing websites is one of my favorite hobbies. It has the additional bonus of making me a bit of money, and it is a skill that could potentially be very useful for my future. I will talk more about this later in Building Passive Income Streams.

Tip #7: Cost of Living AKA Bills

It is really easy to reduce your monthly bills and it is something that can actually make a big difference to how much money you have left-over in your bank account at the end of the month. Essentially, you want to reduce your monthly expenditures to as little as possible in order to pay off your debts as quickly as possible. You are in attack-mode, as Dave Ramsey in *The Total Money Makeover* likes to say. For electricity and gas, obviously you should be doing all the basic things like not turning on all the lights, avoiding the air conditioner and turning on the heat to a minimal level in winter (17 degrees Celsius) and using some warm clothes and blankets to stay warm. Do large loads of laundry occasionally instead of small ones frequently, and hang-dry instead of using the dryer.

For the Internet, check first to see if there are any free signals around your house which you can "borrow." If not, consider getting a smart-phone, or Internet connection at your house, but not both. I have been using my iPhone with unlimited 3G for the past couple years as Internet at my house, with good results. Download speeds are not lightning fast, nor can I stream videos but this does not really matter to me. If I have serious Internet tasks to do, I make a plan to do them at work on my desktop computer with fast Internet. Or, if you want a high speed Internet connection, pay for it at your house but then consider getting a "stupid-phone" that just does texts and calls. Both are unnecessary when you are in attack-mode. Yes, people will think you are a bit strange but you should not worry about that--you have bigger and better things going on! Think about your long-term goal of being financially free.

Tip #8: Plan your Day

One of the fastest ways to spend a lot of money is by being disorganized. For example, maybe you work from nine to five and then you are meeting a friend at seven. You might not have time to go home in between work and your appointment, so you grab a quick meal out. Or, perhaps you work from ten to six but you like to sleep in so you get up at the last second possible and get a cup of coffee and muffin on your way to work. Perhaps you are going to your friend's house for dinner and need to bring a bottle of wine, except you have no time to go to the big supermarket, so you just pick up a bottle at the convenience store. Maybe you meet some friends for a few drinks on a Friday night but you have no idea what time the last subway or bus leaves to get you back home and before you know it, you are spending $20 on a taxi ride.

These are examples of disorganization that cost you money. By planning your day out, you could have avoided getting that dinner out between work and seeing your friend. Another possibility would be to meet the friend later and instead go home for some dinner, or even better, prepare something from home to eat. Waking up fifteen minutes earlier saves money through making coffee at home and eating breakfast which would also probably mean going to bed a bit earlier the night before. Considering the dinner earlier in the week provides time to go to the big supermarket to buy that same bottle of wine for half the price. Better yet, try keeping a few bottles in your cupboard for just that kind of occasion. Finally, make it a priority to know the information about public transportation such as when the last bus or subway leaves and then have the personal discipline to be on it, no matter how much fun you are having.

Tip #9: Clothes and Shopping

Clothes are one area where you can spend almost nothing or your entire monthly salary. My friends make good-natured jokes about how they always see me wearing the same two or three things, and far from being annoyed or upset, it makes me feel quite happy. I only go shopping twice a year, before summer and before winter and I will skip it if I do not feel like

I need anything. You truly do not need to spend a lot of money on clothes and require only a few basics. Here is what my wardrobe usually consists of:

3-4 pairs of work pants (some of which can double as casual wear too), 4-5 work shirts (which I can also wear out casually), a few t-shirts, 2 pairs of jeans, 3 pairs of shorts, 3 sweaters, 2 hoodies, a fleece jacket, rain jacket and warm puffy winter jacket. Besides that, I have a few things like pajama pants, underwear, socks, exercise gear and a few hot/cold weather accessories like hats or mitts, but that is about it.

An idea to consider is buying (if you do not have them already) a few quality items from home. Do some research about the climate in your new country and bring 2 pairs of nice work shoes, 1 pair of casual shoes, 4-5 work shirts, 3-4 pairs of work pants, a nice jacket and sweater (if in a colder climate), and enough underwear, socks, and bras to last you at least 6 months.

Tip #10: What is the Cheapest Option?

All these tips are helpful in order to pursue a frugal lifestyle so you can pay off your debt very quickly, but the best way to attack your debt is to always think about what is the cheapest possible option. When I was paying off my student loans, I did not use a written budget, but lived in a constant frame of mind where I was trying to figure out how to spend the least amount of money. For example, I would consider my options for transportation to go somewhere and choose biking or walking 95% of the time. When considering which cell-phone plan to sign up for I chose the pay-as-you-go $10 per month plan rather than a contract with many extra but unnecessary features that would have added significantly to the total cost. For my vacations, I never thought about a trip abroad, but instead figured out how to spend my time in Korea in a fun, but frugal way such as a day-trip to the beach.

Is It Ever Too Late to Start?

You might be reading this book when you are in your late forties, fifties or even sixties and thinking that your financial landscape is pretty bleak. Perhaps you have lots of debt, including credit cards, no emergency fund and nothing in the way of retirement savings or other assets such as a house. You might even think that it is too late to start and that you should just continue the way that you have been living. While you *have* lost your best years for retirement savings (your twenties and thirties) because you have mostly missed out on the power of compound interest which will make it much harder for you to retire early or at all, it is never too late to put your financial house in order. Here are my top five tips for the older teacher who is just getting started on their journey towards financial freedom.

Top 5 Tips for the Older Teacher

Work Past 65 Assess carefully whether or not you can retire at 65, or whatever age you had in mind. It is not uncommon for people to continue to work past 65, at least part-time. If you want to crunch some numbers for your own situation, check out a "Retirement Withdrawal Calculator."

Get out of Debt It is even more urgent for you to get out of debt than it is for someone who is younger. There is probably no worse scenario for you than to be forced to retire through an illness of some sort and still have debts. This will involve massive sacrifice for a year or two, or however long it takes. You are on *life-support*, financially speaking, so **urgent action is required.**

Rebalance your Portfolio If you do have any investments, now is not the time to be gambling them away. Only invest in blue chip dividend paying stocks and broad market stock or bond ETFs. You should hold a significant portion of bonds the older you get; we will get into more details about investment choices later on in the book.

Consider your Spending Habits Take time to reflect carefully about what spending habits got you into this bad situation in the first place. Too many expensive clothes or electronic toys? Eating out? Flashy cars? Expensive luxury vacations? Poor decisions related to employment? Change your habits or you will never be able to secure your financial future.

Retire "Abroad" It is expensive to live in a place like Canada so consider living somewhere in South-East Asia or South or Central America. A few places to look at would be Thailand, Vietnam, Malaysia, Ecuador or Nicaragua. You could live in any of these places for less than $1,000 a month if you are frugal. But, beware: many of these countries require a certain income level in order to give you a "retirement" visa, so you will need to check this carefully.

Step 4: Advance Your Career

After you have paid off the majority of your debt, it is time to start focusing more on your career and how to improve your employment prospects so you can move up in the world. Teaching English as Second Language is not exactly rocket science and you will most often be teaching pretty basic things to students who often do not have high expectations for their native English speaking teachers. The administration at your place of employment is also likely to have low expectations of you as well. Nevertheless, this should not be an excuse to be lazy or fail to upgrade your qualifications; you should be constantly trying to improve yourself.

I will give you examples of some career behaviours to avoid. I have numerous acquaintances here in Korea who have been working at universities for the past six, eight or ten years. They got their jobs back in the old days when anyone with a bachelor's degree in anything could get the job just by luck, or knowing someone on the inside. During their tenure, they have spent plenty of time at the expat bars, hanging out, or traveling around Asia--basically doing anything besides professional development training to improve their job prospects such as obtaining a CELTA or DELTA certification, getting a related master's degree, learning a second language, getting academic papers published, presenting at conferences, or getting a teaching licence from their home country. Over this long period of rest and relaxation, qualifications for university teachers in Korea have risen, such that it is now almost impossible to get the job without a master's degree and a few years of experience teaching at a university, or at the very least adults or high school students. Now, those people who were just enjoying life, sliding on by with only doing the minimum have started to lose their jobs and are finding it extremely difficult to get another job with similar benefits. Do not find yourself in that situation!

How do you go about improving your skills and qualifications? The first piece of advice that I could give you is to decide whether or not you want to make teaching a longer-term career option. Like many people, perhaps you just came overseas to teach for a bit of adventure and the chance to pay off some debts and save money. If this is the case, do not worry so much about improving your teaching qualifications and instead focus on making a plan for life after teaching. Perhaps you could do some online courses to improve your career prospects once you return home, maybe there is some sort of certification test you could take or you could work on applications to graduate school. Definitely be thinking about your post-teaching life because going home without a plan is the surest way to burn through massive amounts of money and find yourself teaching abroad again when you do not have any options left and are broke and desperate.

If you decide that you like teaching and want to make it a career, then get qualified by doing any of the following:

- complete a master's degree in education, TESOL, or English

- get a CELTA or DELTA certificate

- get certified to administer and grade popular exams such as TOIEC speaking or IELTs

- get a teaching certification and license from your home country, which opens up the option of teaching at international schools

- get published, formally or informally

- make a name for yourself through blogging, social media or other online ventures

- present at conferences and make sure you get certificates proving that you did so

- volunteer with an English teaching organization (for example, KOTESOL) and accept positions with increasing responsibility

Networking

Perhaps the most important advice I can give you about advancing your career in the ESL teaching world is that networking is extremely important. It is a very small world and once you have been in a place for a few years, you will start to know people all around the world, working at interesting jobs in fabulous countries. Keep in touch with people that you meet and then when you look for a job, you will have a network of people to help you. Within your chosen country, networking is also extremely important and I estimate that 50% of jobs (and most of the best ones) are filled through word of mouth and are never advertised.

Student Loans

A quick note for those considering doing a master's degree. Just because you *can* get students loans does not mean that you *should*. **Students loans are NOT free money** and you will eventually have to pay them back. In most countries, you can never clear them, even through bankruptcy. If you are working at a full-time job teaching English, you should be able to fund your program through your regular monthly pay, and although you may not be able to save as much as you want to, it is a far better plan than taking on more debt. If you cannot afford tuition through your regular pay, consider a cheaper program (the best option), or one that will let you pay course by course instead of in big lump-sum payments (an okay option). When you are choosing which master's program to do, make sure that you will have increased earning power upon completion of the program. There is no sense in spending $20,000, $40,000, or even more on a program that will not help you get a better job. Knowledge is a good thing, but there is no sense dropping thousands of dollars on it when there are so many courses and other things available for free online. In addition, it would be wise to pay off your undergraduate loans *before starting another degree*. Always remember: *student loans are not free money* and the fewer of them that you have (or acquire in the future), the sooner you will be financially free. Do not be a slave to debt and make sure you have the power of compound interest working for you, not against you.

Step 5: Build a Full Emergency Fund

Once you have paid off your debts and have started to focus on your career, it is time to build up a full emergency fund of around three to six months of living expenses. If you have children, old and frail pets, health concerns, or sick parents back home and you might need to fly back at a moment's notice, then I recommend closer to six months, which for most people would be around $6,000-$10,000. If you are young, single with no pets or children and have healthy parents then three months ($3,000-$5,000) should be enough. Since you have already paid off all your debts and have a small emergency fund of $2,000, it really should not take you that much time at all to build up a larger amount. You need to keep this money somewhere where it is easily accessible, perhaps half in your home country and half in the country where you are teaching. You could consider a high-interest savings account to earn a bit more on this money, but the primary focus is to have it available in case of emergency and not to make money off of it.

After you pay off your debts and build up your emergency fund, you are well on your way towards financial freedom and you hopefully have mastered the art of frugal living, long-term instead of short-term thinking, and living differently than other people do. It is now time to turn your attention towards investment options, such as dividend paying stocks or ETFs.

A Special Note for Readers New to Investing

For readers new to investing and the stock market I recommend that you read the following resources listed below before starting the next section, Step 6: Save $5,000 and Research Investment Options. There is good news and bad news, but we will go with the bad news first. The bad news is that you have to learn a whole new language, but the good news is that the resources to help you do that can be found for free around the web. Please read the following in order, starting at the top and continuing down the list-they are easy enough to find by searching on Google. For readers who feel that they already have a basic grasp of investing vocabulary, terms, and concepts please dive in and start reading the next section of this book.

1. *Investopedia* - "Stock Basics Tutorial" Be sure to check out all 9 nine parts.

2. *About Money* - "The Complete Beginner's Guide to Investing in Stock" Spend some time scrolling around this helpful site. Hopefully much of the material is now familiar to you from reading the articles over at *Investopedia*.

3. *Vanguard* - "Vanguard's Principles for Investing Success" Some great advice here.

4. *Dividend Monk* - "Dividend Stocks: The Essential Guide" I love dividend paying stocks and they are the only kind that I invest my own money in. The *Dividend Monk* is one of the best financial sites out there, so be sure to read at least the first three articles he lists (although all of them are packed with good information).

5. *Vanguard* - "ETF Investing Can Add Flexibility to your Portfolio" Besides investing in dividend paying stocks, I also like ETFs. Here is a quick primer on what exactly they are and their numerous advantages over mutual funds.

At the back of the book, you will find a wealth of investing and stock market resources including book titles, websites, podcasts, and more. Please take a minute and look at this valuable source of information.

Step 6: Save $5,000 and Research Investment Options

Do your Research

Congratulations! You have probably paid off most of your debts, are well on your way to career success and have a full emergency fund. It is now time to learn about investing options and how to get started with that. Before we discuss the finer points, be aware that the information I am giving you is simply a brief overview of options to consider and you should do your own research, especially as it relates to your country of origin because things like taxes vary from country to country. Also be aware that I am not a certified financial advisor so take my advice (and even that of *certified* financial advisors), mix it up with a good dose of common sense, plenty of your own research, and then come to your own investment decision. Personally, before I ever invested a single dollar in the stock market, I probably spent at least five hundred hours researching and figuring out what strategy I would employ and I recommend that you do the same. If you are new to investing, hopefully you have read the beginner level resources that I recommended in the previous section. For beginners to continue your research and for more advanced investors, a few things for you to check out are:

Investopedia - This website is an excellent resource because it contains easy to understand definitions of common financial terms as well as educational articles.

Fool.com - This website (and its corresponding podcast: *Motley Fool Money*) is a bit more advanced in terms of content but still contains lots of useful advice for the beginner. They take a long-term, investment style approach, which I advocate as well.

Dividend Monk - As you will see later, I LOVE dividend stock investing and this website is by far the best for basic information and dividend stock reports. I will always read what the *Dividend Monk* has to say about a particular stock before purchasing it for my own portfolio. His portfolio is an excellent place to start if you are looking for some investment ideas and you would be well served by basically copying him.

Vanguard - I am a fan of investing in ETFs (Exchange Traded Funds) and this is the best company out there. Their complete listing of ETFs is helpful in seeing the range of options and they also have some useful articles on retirement planning and investment choices.

Why You Need at Least $5,000 to Get Started

During the next half year to a year, you should be saving $5,000 and researching obsessively. Treat it like a full-time job and dedicate yourself seriously to getting informed and knowledgeable about investing. It is something that will benefit you greatly for the rest of your life and you should trust nobody but yourself in this area; the reason for this is that most financial advisors are salespeople who get a commission based on the products that they sell you. I recommend waiting until you have $5,000 to begin investing for the following reasons:

Diversification is a key component of investing. You do not want to have all your eggs in one basket and with less than $5,000, it is simply too hard to diversify without paying too high of a proportion in fees. I remember one of my former coworkers who, when he found out that I was just getting into investing had a serious talk with me and shared all his "wisdom." He told me plenty of bizarre things like that I had to buy shares in round lots (100 shares), that brokerage fees did not really matter, and finally that diversification was not so important because you just had to pick the "winners" (I talk more about "round lots" in the section, Dividend Paying Stocks). He had just lost thousands of dollars when his portfolio, the majority of it in American banks, crashed around 2009/2010 and he panicked and sold low; which was the absolute worst thing he could have done. I asked him why I should be taking his advice about investing when obviously his track record did not really give me any confidence. He failed to see the irony.

Anyway, the moral of this story is that a well-diversified portfolio among many industries and countries, along with a mix of stock and bonds, is the best way to reduce volatility and ensure a good night's sleep. Through proper diversification, the highs will not be as high, but the lows will not be as low. Do not worry too much about all the specifics right now because there is plenty more information on this to come! Look over this article on *Investopedia*, "The Importance of Diversification" if you would like to do some additional reading.

Keeping fees low is a huge factor for investment success. If you have only $1,000, you could buy five stocks, but much of the $200 per stock will be eaten up in trading costs.

Compare that to starting with $5,000 and buying four stocks. Only a very small portion of the $1,000 per stock will go towards trading fees.

Most online discount brokerages will not take your account without a *minimum deposit of around $5,000.* If you *happen to find* a brokerage that will let you get started with less than $5,000, and you invest all your money in one or two single stocks, it is likely going to cause you a *significant amount of stress* as that stock fluctuates on the daily market.

Brokerage Options for Expats

In order to buy stocks or ETFs you will need to go through a **brokerage**, which acts as an intermediary between you and other people who have shares of the stock/ETF that you want to buy, or they want to buy shares of the stock/ETF that you are selling. While you can buy things like mutual funds through a bank, I do not recommend that option for reasons I will explain in the next section, Mutual Funds, ETFs and Individual Stocks. For more specific details about the best brokerage options relevant to your home country, I again recommend Andrew Hallam's Book, *The Global Expatriate's Guide to Investing,* available on *Amazon* because he gives an excellent overview of the pros and cons of each brokerage but I will give you a brief overview here.

Brokerage Options for Non-Americans

Andrew Hallam recommends three brokerages for non-Americans including DBS Vickers, TD Direct Investing and Saxo Capital Markets. **DBS Vickers** allows expats to purchase shares using the Hong Kong, Singapore, Canadian and US exchanges. Hallam recommends purchasing shares on the Hong Kong or Canadian markets as opposed to the American one because if you die, your heirs will avoid capital gains taxes, which will be levied even if you, or your heirs, are not American. Fees for DBS Vickers are quite high with minimum trading costs of $29 per trade. However, this is no monthly minimum fee, nor is there an annual fee.

September 2015 update I've heard rumors that DBS Vickers is no longer allowing people outside of Hong Kong or Singapore to open accounts with them. On their website, they recommend calling or emailing to check about your specific situation.

Another option for non-Americans is **TD Direct Investing International**, while owned by Canada's TD Bank it is based in Luxembourg. Through TD Direct, you have access to eighteen markets worldwide. Unlike DBS Vickers, they charge an annual account fee of 0.2% and their trading costs range from 28-35 Euros or higher.

The final option Hallam recommends is **Saxo Capital Markets**, which is located in multiple locations around the world. You can trade on many exchanges around the world and the minimum trading fee is around $25.

Interactive Brokers is where I hold my personal account and Andrew Hallam calls it the "Dark Horse Winner" with extremely low trading costs and the only stipulation being a minimum commission of $10 per month. So, if you are not an active trader and do not generate $10 worth of trading fees, you will be charged that $10 anyway. They get their pound of flesh one way or the other! However, this monthly minimum fee is waived once you hold $100,000 in your account, but of course, you will still pay a commission if you make any trades. Thus far, I have been extremely happy with Interactive Broker's customer service and trading platforms (their mobile app is excellent) but would caution that is perhaps not for the total beginner as it is more geared to the professional, frequent trader and can get quite complicated if you do not know what you are doing, or do not have someone to show you how to get started the first few times.

The only hesitation about using Interactive Brokers, as opposed to the previous three, would be that it is an American company and you might be charged U.S. Estate taxes upon your death, even if you buy from non-American exchanges. You need to check with an international tax accountant for confirmation on this because even Andrew Hallam does not seem that clear on the rules about this.

Brokerage Options for Americans

Americans should strongly consider using **Vanguard,** which is the world's largest purveyor of ETFs, from which you could easily build your entire portfolio. They have the lowest fees in the industry and do not charge commissions other than the minimal fund expenses (ranging from about 0.1-0.5%). The only drawback is that they do not allow American expats to open accounts, so you should really do this before you head overseas, or if it is too late for you, consider "stretching the truth" a little bit and using a local address (of a relative perhaps?) to open an account (but of course, you should never break the law so make your own decision about this one).

Schwab, like Vanguard, is also an excellent choice for American expats but you will also need to have an American address on record so open an account with them before you head overseas. You can buy individual stocks on the US exchanges, as well as Schwab's own ETFs, which you will not pay commission for.

Mutual Funds, ETFs, Bonds and Individual Stocks

When you are investing your first $5,000, you have four basic choices including mutual funds, stock ETFs, bond ETFs, and individual stocks. All of these options are good, except for mutual funds which have no upside and just leave you with less money in your pocket at the end of the day.

Why Mutual Funds are Terrible

Mutual Funds traditionally have been a popular way to enter the stock market and get some "professional" money-management experience as well as diversification. For example, many people only buy one or two mutual funds for their entire portfolio but that portfolio could contain hundreds of stocks. According to *Investopedia*, a **mutual fund** is:

> "An investment vehicle that is made up of a pool of funds collected from many investors for the purpose of investing in securities such as stocks, bonds, money market instruments and similar assets. Mutual funds are operated by money managers, who invest the fund's capital and attempt to produce capital gains and income for the fund's investors. A mutual fund's portfolio is structured and maintained to match the investment objectives stated in its prospectus.
>
> One of the main advantages of mutual funds is that they give small investors access to professionally managed, diversified portfolios of equities, bonds and other securities, which would be quite difficult (if not impossible) to create with a small amount of capital. Each shareholder participates proportionally in the gain or loss of the fund. Mutual fund

units, or shares, are issued and can typically be purchased or redeemed as needed at the fund's current net asset value (NAV) per share, which is sometimes expressed as NAVPS."

Prior to 2010, ETFs did not exist and therefore mutual funds, although they were not a great product (and are still not great!), were the best that people could do apart from buying individual stocks. There are two reasons why I do not like mutual funds and why I would never recommend that anyone use them as a means to prepare for their retirement: active management and high loads. I will talk about them in turn.

Reason #1: Active Management

Reason number one is that most mutual funds are actively managed, as opposed to passively managed, which means that the manager of the fund is buying and selling with sometimes alarming frequency. The problem with frequent trading within a mutual fund is the same problem that the individual investor has with too frequent trading: the expenses are just too high. Statistics show that in a random ten year period, about 70% of mutual funds under-perform their corresponding passive index and that number increases to 80% for a twenty year period. If you are unsure what I mean by "under-performing" the corresponding passive index, I will give you an example.

If you want to invest in the five hundred biggest companies in the USA, you could buy the ETF with the ticker symbol SPY (SPDR S&P 500 ETF). The way this ETF works is that it passively buys the companies in the S&P 500 index at approximately the same ratios as the index itself and your performance will be essentially the same as that underlying index because the fees you pay are only 0.11% per year, which is astoundingly low. Depending on what brokerage you use, your commission to buy and sell this ETF could be as low as two to three dollars.

Or, you could buy a mutual fund such as Fidelity Large Cap Stock Fund (FLCSX) which invests in basically the same things as SPY (look at the top 20 holdings in both and you will see the same companies, almost without exceptions), except that you will pay a fee of 0.88% per year. While you may be able to buy some funds without a commission fee (such as buying "in-house" funds through your brokerage, especially if it is with a big bank), there are still large commissions in many cases, especially for Canadians. Clearly, it is far better to buy the ETF with a fee of 0.11% per year instead of the mutual fund that charges 0.88%, to say nothing of commissions and other fees associated with mutual funds which are almost always higher than with ETFs. Check out this article from *CBS Money Watch,* "Why "Active" Investment is a Losing Bet."

If you are from Canada, the news is even worse. Canadians are lucky to be living in a safe, prosperous country but one area that they trail the rest of the developed world is in mutual fund fees. There's an article from the *Financial Post* which shows that Canadians pay an average of 2.2% per year in mutual funds fees, compared with an average of 0.95% for seventeen other developed countries. If the mutual fund gains 7% that year and your fees are 2%, you will only see 5% of that return. It is basically throwing away money, every year for the entire time that you own that fund.

Reason #2: High Loads

Reason number two why mutual funds are bad news is **loads** that you have to pay when you buy or sell them (www.investopedia.com/terms/l/loadfund.asp has details about what **mutual fund loads** are). These loads can eat up your profits significantly and hamper your total return. People that work at banks or even some investment "advisors" are sales people more so than they are advisors. They get paid by selling you funds which their banks own or funds which have some sort of partnership with the investment advisor. These loads can be extremely high--up to five percent. It is actually a disgrace to the entire financial advising industry that these fees are so high. As you can see, the deck is stacked against you if you choose to invest in mutual funds and you do so at the peril of your financial future. Thankfully, there are far better options available to you in the form of ETFs or individual stocks. It should be noted, there are some companies who offer low or no-load mutual funds such as Vanguard, so if you do buy them, go with a company that offers this.

Stock and Bond ETFs: Excellent Alternatives to Mutual Funds

With the introduction of ETFs around 2010, the investing landscape became much friendlier for the average investor. According to *Investopedia,* **ETFs** are:

"A security that tracks an index, a commodity or a basket of assets like an index fund, but trades like a stock on an exchange. ETFs experience price changes throughout the day as they are bought and sold. Because it trades like a stock, an ETF does not have its net asset value (NAV) calculated every day like a mutual fund does. By owning an ETF, you get the diversification of an index fund as well as the ability to sell short, buy on margin and purchase as little as one share. Another advantage is that the expense ratios for most ETFs are lower than those of the average mutual fund. When buying and selling ETFs, you have to pay the same commission to your broker that you'd pay on any regular order."

I started investing in the stock market around 2009, which was the point when ETFs were just entering the market but had not become popular yet. When I was researching about investing a couple of years before that, there was almost no mention of them at all, which was why I ended up investing in a portfolio of around twenty dividend paying stocks. For those who like to be a bit more active in their investing by researching companies and making decisions about what stocks to buy, buying individual stocks can be a good way to go: however for the majority of people who want to invest and forget about it, I strongly recommend using ETFs. You can literally check your account once or twice a year and spend only an hour or two each time. Perfect for busy people!

If you like the idea of investing made easy, there are two ETF portfolios that I would recommend. The first is for the *younger investor* (18-45) and the second for the *older investor* (46+), along with recommendations for *Americans* and *non-Americans* in each age group. You can easily buy ETFs just as you would individual stocks by opening up a brokerage account (refer back to Brokerage Options for Expats for advice on how to open an account). I recommend a combination of stocks and bonds, going heavier on stocks the younger that you are and heavier on bonds the older you get. The theory is that bonds and stocks tend to counterbalance each other; when the value of stocks goes up, bonds often go down and vice-versa. It is generally thoughts that bonds are more "stable" since they do not fluctuate as much as stocks so the older you get, the more stability you want, which comes through buying more bonds. Of course, this stability comes at a price as bonds have under-performed stocks over the long haul (**under-perform** = have lower annual rates of return). In addition, you want to be more focused on "income" instead of "growth" as you get older, which is another reason why you would want to invest more heavily in bonds the older that you get.

You *Can* Lose Money with Bonds

A quick note about buying bond ETFs. The absolute worst time to buy them is in a rising interest rate environment (interest rates are increasing) because the share price of the ETF will go nowhere but down. Conversely, in a declining interest rate environment, the share price of bond ETFs will go up. While you will still get the interest payments credited to your account no matter what, if you sell the bond ETF when interest rates are rising, you could actually lose money. In 2015, interest rates are at historic lows and will certainly be increasing in the next few years, so it might be prudent to ease into bonds during the next 1-5 years, instead of putting significant amounts of money all at once into them right now. Take a look at this article on *Investopedia*, "Top 8 Ways to Lose Money on Bonds."

Younger Investors: Americans

If you are American, I strongly recommend opening up an account with Vanguard before you go overseas and buying ETFs exclusively through them. They are the industry leader in terms of low fees and selection. Here is what your portfolio could look like:

70%: VT (Total World Stock-US and International)

10%: BND (Total Bond Market-US)

10%: BNDX (Total International Bond)

10%: VWO (FTSE Emerging Markets)

It is very easy to decide where to put additional money--just check the ratios using a bit of simple math (ideally 70-10-10-10) and find whatever ETF is out of balance. If that ETF is lower than the allotted percentage then that is where you should add money. If it is higher, you do not have to do anything--just avoid adding additional money to it (selling to rebalance your portfolio just increases trading costs and is unnecessary if you are adding more money and buying). The theory is that by adding money to the lowest percentage, you will be buying what has been under-performing and it will be cheap, as opposed to whatever has a high percentage which will be over-performing and relatively expensive.

For example (we'll assume that the initial investment amount is $10,000 for the sake of simplicity):

January, Year 1 - You have $10,000 and buy $7,000 VT, $1,000 BND, $1,000 BNDX, and $1,000 VWO (70-10-10-10 ratio).

July, Year 1 - You have been saving your money from the day job and have an additional $5,000 to invest. The stock market has been doing well, but the bond market has been lagging.

   Current values of your ETFs are: $8,000 VT, $500 BND, $500 BNDX, and $1,000 VWO

   Buy: $2,500 VT, $1,000 BND, $1,000 BND, and $500 VWO

   New totals: $10,500 VT, $1,500 BND, $1,500 BNDX, and $1,500 WVO, which fits the 70-   10-10-10 ratio

January, Year 2 - You have been continuing to save money and now have an additional $5,000 to invest. Emerging markets and the bond markets have done well, but the total world stock market is lagging a bit.

   Current values are: $9,000 VT, $2,000 BND, $2,000 BNDX, and $2,000 VWO

   Buy: $5,000 VT

   New totals: $14,000 VT, $2,000 BND, $2,000 BNDX, and $2,000 VWO

July, Year 2 - You have been doing some extra work these past few months and now have an additional $10,000 to invest. Bonds have been lagging significantly, but stocks have been doing well.

   Current values are: $17,000 VT, $1,500 BND, $1,500 BNDX, and $3,000 VWO

   Buy: $6,000 VT, $2000 BND, $2,000 BNDX, and $0 VWO

   New totals: $23,000 VT, $3,500 BND, $3,500 BNDX, and $3,000 VWO

   As you can see, it takes nothing more than very basic math skills and less than a couple hours of your time per year. It does not have to be exact, especially if you are paying high fees ($20+ per transaction) when you buy shares--but you should try to stay within a few percentage points of your plan. If you are paying large commissions, simply put your new money into only one or two of the ETFs and not three or four. This should bring everything into a reasonable balance and not cost you too much in trading costs.

Younger Investors: Non-Americans

Remember that non-Americans should avoid investing on the US exchanges because if they die, their heirs will get hit with a hefty estate tax upon their death for any assets over $60,000 US. However, it is possible to use Vanguard and iShares Canada to construct a similar portfolio to the American one. If you are not Canadian, it is possible to construct a similar portfolio using ETFs from your own country's stock exchange, although you will have to do a bit of research.

70%: XWD (iShares MSCI World Stock)

10%: VBU (US Aggregate Bond)

10%: VBG (Global ex-US Aggregate Bond)

10%: VEE (FTSE Emerging Markets)

Just follow the above example for Americans on how to rebalance your portfolio semi-annually or annually.

Older Investors: Americans

When you are young, growth should be your focus and the best way to get significant growth in your portfolio is by holding a large percentage of it in stocks and a smaller proportion in bonds (in the previous two cases for younger investors: 80% stocks, 20% bonds). However, this higher growth does not come without a cost in the form of higher volatility, which means that you might experience a significant drop in the value of your portfolio in a single year, month or even a day. You should not lose sleep over this because the idea is that since you are young and your money will be invested in the markets for twenty years or more, you will be able to ride the yearly fluctuations up and down without having to sell. It depends on what index of stocks you are talking about, but historically the market has returned seven to ten percent per year over the long-term.

As you get older and closer to retirement age, you are less able to safely ride these huge fluctuations that come with a large proportion of stocks in your portfolio and so you should move towards more bonds and other instruments that produce income since you are not so worried about growth as you would be if you were younger.

Here is a sample portfolio for an American aged 46 or older:

60%: VT (Total World Stock-US and International)

20%: BND (Total Bond Market-US)

10%: BNDX (Total International Bond Market)

10%: VWOB (Emerging Markets Government Bond)

As you contribute more of your salary to your portfolio, just rebalance it to bring the percentages up to their allotted values; do not actually sell anything until you are forced to in retirement. As you move into your 60's and 70's, you could even increase the proportion of bonds and your portfolio might look something like this: 40% VT, 20% BND, 20% BNDX, and 20% VWOB.

In your 60's or 70's, you are probably not contributing more money to your portfolio, but ideally are living off of the income you have generated through this portfolio, in which case you would withdraw the distributions or dividend payments from your brokerage account every few months as necessary but would try not to sell any shares.

If you have to sell some shares, use whatever ETF is the highest proportion surplus, which means that it has done well in the past few months or year since you rebalanced your portfolio. Whatever you do, do not sell from whatever has the lowest percentage relative to what you want it to be since in effect, you would be selling low.

Older Investors: Non-Americans

All of the advice mentioned above for older American investors is applicable to you (the non-American), except that you will want to avoid the US Stock Market. If you are Canadian, your portfolio could look something like:

60%: XWD (iShares MSCI World Stock)

15%: VBU (US Aggregate Bond)

15%: VBG (Global ex-US Aggregate Bond)

10%: VDY (FTSE Canadian High Dividend Yield)

As you move into your 60's and 70's, it might look more like this:

40% XWD, 25% VBU, 25% VBG, and 10% VDY

Dividend Paying Stocks: also a Good Alternative to Mutual Funds

As I mentioned before in the previous section about ETFs, I began investing before they were popular and the strategy I decided on was individual, dividend paying stocks from mostly big, blue chip companies. Both ETFs and individual stocks are much better options than mutual funds because you will pay a lot less money in fees; the money you make will go into your pocket and not fund some mutual fund manager's luxury yacht. Investing in dividend paying stocks is perfect for those who are interested in financial things and want to put the time in to research companies. It is a more active approach to investing than using indexes through ETFs in that you are choosing individual companies. If simple and easy is more your style, and you like the idea of spending only an hour or two a year figuring out your investments, refer back to the previous section on using ETFs and stick with that. You really cannot go wrong with either choice, when done for the long-term. Before we started with the in-depth details about dividend stock investing, I recommend reading "Dividend Stocks: The Essential Guide," from *The Dividend Monk* if you have not done so already.

Blue chips and dividends might be too much jargon which you do not understand if you are new to investing. **Dividends** are a portion of the company's earnings that are paid out to the shareholders (me or you!) at various times throughout the year, usually quarterly (4 times a year). These dividends get deposited directly into your brokerage account. A **shareholder** is someone who owns a share (a portion) of a certain company. **Blue chips** are big, mature companies with household names that you would recognize and usually produce consistent profits year after year (for example: Pfizer, Chevron, McDonalds or Coca-Cola). They may not be growing a lot since it is hard for such big companies to have huge amounts of growth but consistency is their strong point and they often produce moderate, but growing dividends year after year.

If you are American, simply open a brokerage account with a company like Schwab,

49

Interactive Brokers or Sogotrade and buy stocks on the American exchanges. If you are not American, it is more complicated. While it is simple enough to open a brokerage account with a company like Interactive Brokers, or TD Direct International and invest in American companies, your heirs will pay estate taxes on investments over $60,000 to the American government upon your death, whether or not any of you are American. The international brokerages such as TD Direct, DBS Vickers and some of the American ones such as Interactive Brokers allow trading on various exchanges around the world, not only the American ones. On Interactive Brokers, you can buy stocks from Canada, India, Germany, and South Korea to name just a few examples. So it is possible to limit yourself to less than $60,000 in American companies and then buy stocks from non-American exchanges. The major problem with this is that a majority of the world's biggest companies are American and by buying only Canadian companies, for example, you are getting a very small slice of the world's pie, which is a pretty dangerous endeavour due to lack of diversification. One possibility to get around this issue is by finding American companies which are listed on other exchanges. Another option is to buy up to $60,000 in American stocks and then purchase stocks or ETFs from other exchanges. There are a lot of quality, blue chip dividend paying stocks on the Canadian and European exchanges: the big 4 Canadian banks, European telecoms, and oil companies just to name a few examples. Again, it is quite complicated and you should consult an international tax accountant before making any big decisions. It can be somewhat expensive at between $50-100 per hour, but it is worth it to help you avoid the worst tax mistakes that can cost you a lot more.

Five Basic Principles of Dividend Stock Investing

The **first principle** behind dividend stock investing is that you build a portfolio of stocks which *pay consistent and growing dividends*. You keep buying more stocks, with money from your day job and also by re-investing the dividend payments so that eventually you are able to live off the dividends in retirement without actually selling any of the stocks.

The **second principle** is that you should only buy stock from companies that you are comfortable holding for the next twenty or thirty years and preferably, forever. You are *investing, not trading.* **Investing** is buying stocks that you think will do well *long-term* and

50

holding them for a long period of time. **Trading** is buying stocks that you hope will rise quickly in the *short-term* and trying to profit on that by selling them (buying companies that you hope will lose money in the short-term and then selling them to make profits is known as shorting stocks, but that is a very advanced level investing technique that carries significant risks which you should not engage in).

The **third principle** is to *buy low*. If you hold the stocks for a long period of time it does not matter all that much when you buy it, but it is still nice to get a deal. For example, if you buy an expensive sweater at full price and wear it 500 times, it does not really matter how much you paid for it. However, if you could have gotten that sweater for half price, then it is an even better value. I will talk about how to "buy low" in the next section, How to Choose Which Stocks to Buy.

What about when stocks are at record highs and you want to begin investing? It certainly is not an enviable position to be in, but all is not lost. If you had begun investing after the crash of 2009, you should have been selling everything but the kids to get some extra cash and buying whatever stocks you could get your hands on. It was like everything in your favorite store was half price! When stocks are expensive, you can invest gradually over time, instead of in one lump-sum. This method is called **dollar cost averaging** and there are various studies showing that investors who use this method actually do better than those who try to **time the market** (timing the market is when you try to guess the market highs and sell at that point and conversely, the market lows when you want to buy, but even professional money managers have a dismal record of predicting this). If you had $50,000 to invest, you could invest $5,000 per month for the next ten months, but if the stock market has a significant drop during that time, be prepared to abandon the plan and use whatever remaining money you have immediately. While buying low is ideal, if you do not, it does not really make that much difference when investing for the long-term (10 years or more), so do not let it cause you too much stress.

The **fourth principle** is related to the third and it is to always keep in the mind the *idea of fear and greed.* If you follow the financial headlines to any degree, you will observe the following rules:

When the stock market goes up, up, up--people buy, buy, buy. They are greedy and want to get in on the action.

When the stock market crashes--people sell, sell, sell. They are fearful and worried that they will lose even more money.

You need to manage your fear and greed, and act in an opposite way to the herd. When the market is going up, just hold on to what you already have--do not throw extra money into the market to get an additional piece of the action. Just wait patiently. What goes up must come down. When the market crashes, do not worry about your total account value. Just have the attitude that everything in your favorite store is now on sale and you should be buying everything on your wish list. Throw all your extra money into the market and be buying when everyone else is selling. Managing your emotions and not following the crowd are key principles to stock investing success and they could be applied to ETF investing as well.

Finally, you want to buy stocks from companies with a *history of increasing their dividends,* year after year after year. The company with the highest dividend might not necessarily by the best option for you because they are perhaps funding this dividend not out of earnings but by some sketchy maneuvering like issuing more shares or going into debt. Keep reading--I will talk more about the finer details of choosing which stocks to buy in the next section.

How to Choose Which Stocks to Buy

If you have decided to buy individual dividend paying stocks as opposed to mutual funds (I hope so!) or ETFs (a good option too), here is some basic advice to help you choose your companies. If you are going to invest in ETFs, $5,000 is enough to get started because an ETF, by its very nature is diversified. However, my general rule if you are going to buy individual stocks is that you should have at least $10,000 to invest, in which case you would choose four stocks. When you are getting started, a good rule of thumb is to buy about $2,500 worth of each stock because you will keep your trading costs low but will get some degree of diversification. Some people advocate only buying **round lots** (an order for 100 shares), but some stocks are very expensive (Google for example) and the average investor would be unable to do this. Simply buy $2,500 worth of each stock and do not worry about how many shares you are getting (details about actually executing an order to buy or sell will be discussed in the next chapter, Invest in the Financial Markets). The actual share price is meaningless as it relates to investing so do not let it be a factor in your decision making process. A company with a share price of $500 is no "better" or "worse" than a company with a $5 share price, based on that factor alone.

When choosing stocks for your portfolio, start by examining lists like the Dividend Aristocrats, which are companies that have raised their dividends every year for the past 25 years and are on the S&P 500 index. Dividend champions have similarly raised their dividends for the same period of time but are not included in the S&P 500 index. You can also find these lists for other countries besides the USA. Simply search for something like "Dividend aristocrats + country." You can look at portfolios of dividend stock investors like myself (keep reading), or *The Dividend Monk*. Once you have a few ideas, it is time to do some more research. An excellent place to start is *The Dividend Monk* and his very helpful stock analysis reports. He has reviewed almost all of the American dividend paying stocks that you might consider buying and his recommendations should be taken very seriously. Beyond that, you should do your own research and consider the following factors that you can find on *Yahoo Finance* by looking at the "key statistics" and the "historical prices" for each stock.

By using *Yahoo Finance*, it is very simple to compare a list of stocks. Sign into your *Yahoo* account (or make one), then go to **My Portfolio** and **Create Portfolio**. Enter the symbols for the stocks that you want to compare which you have found through sample portfolios from other dividend stock investors, or through the dividend aristocrats and champions' lists. Just use the **Default View** for now because you can easily adjust it later. Then when you are able to see your stock list, click on **Customize View,** to add and remove fields so that you can easily compare whatever you want. I usually include: (dividend) yield, EPS EST current year, EPS EST next year, P/E, P/E next year, and PEG Ratio. Do not worry if you are unfamiliar with these variables and acronyms--I will explain them in the next section

The Key Metrics I Look at

Earnings Per Share The EPS for the current year (ESP EST current year) is not so important on its own, but only has value when compared with the estimate for the next year. The estimate for the next year should be higher than the current year because it is a sign that the company is making an increasing amount of money. If it is the same, or a bit lower it is not a huge problem, but if it is significantly lower it can warrant a closer examination as to why this is the case.

Increasing Dividend Yield This is very easy to find on *Yahoo Finance* by searching for a company and then looking at the main page that comes up. For example, at the time of writing this book (early 2015) Exxon Mobil (XOM) has a yield of 2.76/share, or 3.1% at the current stock price. This means that for each share you own, you will get paid $2.76 per year, assuming no dividend cuts or increases. If you own 100 shares, you will make $276 in dividends that year. The percentage will go up as the stock price goes down and conversely, down as the stock price goes up, but you will get your $2.76/share regardless of the stock price. I generally look for stocks that have a yield of between two and five percent (greater than 5% can sometimes signal danger due to a high payout ratio--keep reading) and a history of increasing dividends. The dividend history is easy to find by going to *Yahoo Finance,* entering the ticker symbol for the company you are interested in, and clicking on **historical prices** and then **dividends only** and searching back ten or twenty years. While a dividend cut, or no increase for a year or two is not necessarily terrible, there should be a good reason for it such as an acquisition of another company, an oil spill (BP!) or a significant reduction of debt.

Payout Ratio Closely related to the dividend yield is the **payout ratio** which is found on *Yahoo Finance* under **key statistics**. For example, Exxon Mobil has a payout ratio of 33%, which means that it pays out $0.33 for every dollar of net income that it makes. The rest goes to other things such as paying off debt, savings, share buybacks or investing back into the company for future growth. A payout ratio of 20-50% is ideal because it means that while the company is serious about returning money to shareholders (in the form of dividends), it is not coming at the expense of future growth or through sketchy operating procedures. A payout ratio of more than 50% can signal danger because it means that the company is simply paying too much money out to shareholders and is not investing in the company's future. A payout ratio of more than 100%, no matter what the yield is, is something that you need to avoid at all costs. They are funding the dividend through one of two ways: issuing more shares, which dilutes the ones that you own or by debt. Of course we know that debt is not a good thing, for people or for companies and diluted shares will result in lower share prices in the long-term which means that you will lose money if you decide to sell the stock.

Price to Earnings Ratio The next thing that I look at is the P/E (price to earnings) ratio. According to *Investopedia*, the P/E ratio is:

"A valuation ratio of a company's current share price compared to its per-share earnings. Calculated as: Market Value per Share/Earnings per Share (EPS).

For example, if a company is currently trading at $43 a share and earnings over the last 12 months were $1.95 per share, the P/E ratio for the stock would be 22.05 ($43/$1.95)."

There are various ways to compute the P/E ratio, but there are only two things you need to worry about: the **Trailing P/E** and the **Forward P/E**. Trailing is calculated based on the previous year's earnings and forward is calculated based on the next year's predicted earnings. Of the two, I prefer the *forward P/E* because I am more concerned about a company's future earnings potential than I am with their past. Historically, the average P/E ratio of all the companies in the US since the 1870's has been about fifteen. Very crudely, if a company has a forward P/E of less than fifteen, it can be considered *cheap* and more than fifteen is *expensive*. It is helpful to compare the stock in question's P/E ratio with competitors in the same industry. For example, if I wanted to buy Exxon Mobil, I would also look at Chevron and Conoco Phillip's P/E ratios. Currently, Exxon Mobil has a forward P/E of 15.90 while Apple's is 13.18, which is a very crude indication that Apple is 'cheaper' than Exxon. However, some mature industries such as energy have lower average P/E ratios than companies with high growth like technology, so while P/E should be a metric you look at, it does not give the complete picture of whether or not a stock is a good value.

Price to Earnings Growth Perhaps a more helpful metric than the P/E ratio is the PEG ratio, which takes into account future growth of the company. According to *Investopedia*,

PEG is:

"A stock's price-to-earnings ratio divided by the growth rate of its earnings for a specified time period. The price/earnings to growth (PEG) ratio is used to determine a stock's value while taking the company's earnings growth into account, and is considered to provide a more complete picture than the P/E ratio. The lower the PEG ratio, the more the stock may be undervalued given its earnings performance. The calculation is as follows: P/E ratio ÷ Annual EPS Growth.

The PEG ratio that indicates an over or underpriced stock varies by industry and by company type, though a broad rule of thumb is that a PEG ratio below 1 is desirable."

As of December 2014, Exxon Mobil has a PEG ratio of 3.58, while Apple's is 1.26, which very crudely indicates that Apple is 'cheaper' than Exxon Mobil based on price, earnings and growth.

What I Hold in My Portfolio: Stocks and ETFs

Stocks

Energy: COP-Conoco Phillips, CVX-Chevron, XOM-Exxon Mobil

Industrials: PG-Proctor and Gamble, MMM-3M Company, BA-Boeing Airlines

Financials: BMO-Bank of Montreal, BRK-B-Berkshire Hathaway, SAN-Banco Santander

Technology: AAPL-Apple, INTC-Intel

Consumer Products: MCD-McDonalds, KO-Coca-Cola, KMB-Kimberly Clark

Pharmaceuticals/Medical: JNJ-Johnson & Johnson, PFE-Pfizer, MDT-Medtronic

Telecom: TEF-Telefonica

ETFs

VEE - Vanguard FTSE Emerging Markets

XHY - iShares US High Yield Bond

PFF - iShares US Preferred Stock

GLD - SPDR Gold Shares

SLV - iShares Silver Trust

Trading vs. Investing

There is a subtle, but important difference between *trading* and *investing,* which you should always keep in mind as you decide where and how to enter the stock market, either through individual stocks or ETFs. **Trading** is something you do with a *short duration* of time in mind, while **investing** is something that you do for a much *longer duration*. Short and long durations of time vary from financial guru to financial guru, but Suze Orman, a well-respected financial advisor and author says that if you will need the money within five years, you actually have no business putting it into the stock market and she actually prefers at least ten years. I tend to agree with her. If you will need the money within the next five years (perhaps to go to grad school or put a down payment on a house), and invest it in the stock market for that duration, it is actually *trading*--which is basically *gambling*. Sure, the stock market could go up during that time, but it could also go down significantly, like in 2009. Maybe you "invested" your money in the stock market in 2005 and planned to go to grad school in late 2009. In this case, you would have been much better off simply parking your money in a high interest bank account.

Over the long haul, the stock market will go up, but you need to be able to ride out the short-term fluctuations, which you cannot do if you need the money for something urgent in the next few years. When you invest your money, think of it as ***inaccessible basically until retirement.*** If you want to save for some shorter term things such as grad school or a house, set up a separate savings account (preferably high interest) or something like a 1 year GIC (guaranteed investment certificate) and do not gamble your money away by trading. Day trading may look cool in the movies, but remember that very few people actually make any money doing this and you are competing against supercomputers with algorithms designed by geniuses so the chances of you beating them at this game are slim to none. Just avoid it!

Fundamental vs. Technical Analysis

There are two basic ways to evaluate stocks, **fundamental analysis** and **technical analysis**. **Fundamental analysis** looks at things like profits from year to year and whether they are increasing or decreasing, debt and the ability of the company to pay it off, and also key ratios such as the price to earnings (P/E) or price to earnings growth (PEG). It is focused on the *long-term* prospects of the company.

Technical analysis looks solely at the chart of the stock price over a certain period of time, usually less than a year, and tries to predict the direction of the future stock price based on that. If you are *investing for the long-term* instead of *trading in the short-term*, fundamental analysis is much more useful to you than technical analysis and you should not worry too much about it.

I will tell you a story to illustrate this. I had a co-worker many years ago who paid over a thousand dollars to attend some "investing" seminar when she was back home in the USA over winter vacation. She got back to Korea and was really excited about all the money that she was going to make, simply by making a few trades a day in just minutes (based on technical analysis). She told me about how the instructor pulled up a few charts during their session and made something like $20,000 on the spot. She had these three binders full of complicated formulas and examples which I could make no sense of. I asked her to explain the basics of it because I just did not understand. She could not and needless to say, she did not even attempt to use this program to make any money in the stock market. I do not think she even got as far as opening up a brokerage account. It was just too complicated and confusing for any regular sort of person to understand. If anyone is trying to sell you some sort of program to make quick money using technical analysis--buyer beware. If that person was truly successful at using their program, they would be a multi-millionaire by now and they would not have to scam people like me or you, a few hundred or a thousand dollars at a time.

I'm Scared of the Stock Market!

Something that I hear from my friends and family members all the time is that they are scared of the stock market because they perceive it as too risky for them to put their hard-earned money into. They think that if they invest in stocks, the market is bound to go down and they will lose all their money. They wonder why they cannot keep their money in something like a government bond, GIC (guaranteed investment certificate) or high-interest savings account. The short answer is: *inflation*, which I find far scarier than investing in the markets. *Investopedia* defines **inflation** as:

> "A sustained increase in the general level of prices for goods and services. It is measured as an annual percentage increase. As inflation rises, every dollar you own buys a smaller percentage of a good or service."

Inflation in any country varies from year to year, but it is quite normal for it to be around two to three percent. These days, interest rates are at historically low rates and as you might have noticed, you basically get nothing keeping your money in a regular bank account. If inflation that year is two percent, you are in effect losing two percent on whatever money you have parked in a bank account. It is certainly not as "safe" as it appears to be since you are consistently losing money year after year after year as long as interest rates remain low and inflation rates are average or high.

Of course, you could get a slightly higher interest rate if you lock your money in for a certain period of time like in a GIC or bond; the greater the time you commit the money, the higher the interest rate. These days though, it is still pretty tough to beat inflation, even when locking your money in for terms as long as five or ten years. You also have an additional danger if you lock your money in for such a long period--interest rates are sure to rise in the next few years because they have nowhere to go but up and if you try to withdraw your money earlier, you will face all sorts of penalties. Do you really want to be holding onto something like a ten year GIC with a two percent interest rate when five years from now, the rates for high interest bank accounts have gone up to four percent? It is a pretty terrible situation to find yourself in.

Let's go back to the original question of whether the stock market is "safe," or not. It is not, but you are not any "safer" when you put your money into some sort of low-interest earning account due to inflation. This is a guaranteed loss for you. In the short-term, the stock market may go down but over the long-haul it is almost a guaranteed winner. According to Andrew Hallam, from 1926 to 2013, the US stock market averaged a total annual return of 9.92%. **Total annual return** is the increase in stock price + dividend payments per year, reported as a percentage. For example, if you had $100,000 invested in the stock market and your return for the previous year was 9.92%, your portfolio would be worth $109,920. Nobody can predict the future, but if the past is any indication, if you hold stocks for a long period of time (10+ years) it is pretty hard to lose. Check out this article from *Time Magazine* "How You Slowly Lose Money with Bank Accounts," for more details.

I should add a short warning note about GICs. If you are reading this book far into the future, or there is some sort of crazy maneuvering by the powers that be (mainly the US central bank) and interest rates are reasonably high (perhaps five or six percent for a ten year GIC), I would consider moving a good portion of my portfolio into something like this. For the next few years it seems very unlikely to happen, however, so waiting and wishing for high interest rates on GICs is probably not the best strategy for any of us.

What about Gold and Silver?

I remember quite a few years ago when I worked with two guys who were obsessed with buying gold and silver. They were totally and completely convinced that stockpiling these two assets physically was the best way to put their hard-earned dollars to work. I recall thinking that this seemed like a complicated endeavor because you had to go buy the product and hope you were not getting ripped off. Furthermore, gold and silver require storage sites somewhere and paying for that too. Finally, time, energy, and possibly more costs are likely to appear while searching for someone to buy the products along with hoping they will give you a fair price too. These days, it is easier than ever to invest in gold and silver *without having to hold the physical product* by buying ETFs such as GLD (gold) or SLV (silver). Most of these ETFs have an expense ratio of about 0.4-0.5%, which is higher than many other ETFs; however you need to remember that they actually buy the product and store it, so they *do* have additional costs associated with that. When contemplating the addition of some gold and silver in your portfolio, I *strongly* recommend using ETFs instead of buying the product yourself. It is just far simpler and quite likely cheaper by the time you pay commissions and storage costs.

Overall, I am neutral on gold and silver, and hold a very small portion of both in my own portfolio (about 1% for each). The biggest positive to owning them is increased diversification. When stock prices are tumbling and panic is high, people like to hold onto a physical product such as gold or silver, which increases demand and in turn increases prices. In addition, in countries like China and India, there is a rising demand due to an expanding middle class so prices seem like they will go up, especially for gold over the long-term.

There are numerous negatives to gold and silver as investments but the main ones are historical return rates and lack of earnings and dividends. According to one article, if you went back in time almost 200 years and invested $10,000 into each of stocks, bonds and gold, then adjusted the returns for inflation, today you would have: $5,600,000,000 (stocks), $8,000,000 (bonds) and $26,000 (gold). It is evident that gold is not the best choice.

The reason that gold and silver do not perform well over the long-term, is that they have no intrinsic value of their own and they do not produce a good or service. The price of these commodities is based solely on what people are willing to pay for them while the share price of companies, over the long-term is based on their earnings; it is important to remember the price/earnings ratio (P/E) generally finds an equilibrium of around fifteen, so if a company's earnings keep going up, year after year, the stock price is bound to follow over the long-term. Of course, without earnings, gold and silver are unable to pay a dividend, which is important to you in retirement, where you will hopefully be able to live off these payments. Buying a small amount of either or both of these goods is not a terrible way to diversify, but do not make it a large part of your investment strategy and certainly do not buy more than two or three percent of each of them for your portfolio. Your money can be put to use in much more useful ways, such as in stock and bond ETFs, or dividend paying stocks. All of these things can offer you better returns on your money than gold or silver.

What about Pension Schemes?

Pension schemes offered to teachers abroad are on the whole terrible and make an even worse "investment" choice than mutual funds. Most of these schemes are basically mutual funds at their cores but have far, far higher fees and offer no additional benefits corresponding with these fees for you, the teacher. I hesitate to even call them investments because all they will really do is fleece you of your hard-earned cash and line the pockets of the salespeople. Andrew Hallam spends about half of his book, *The Global Expatriate's Guide to Investing* espousing the evils of them. You can also read about this in a shorter article of his, "What International Teachers and Their Administrators Need to Know about Investing."

Maybe I will Just Depend on the Government in Retirement

During my time abroad, I have encountered more than a few expats teaching English who, despite having taught abroad for years have nothing more in their bank accounts than enough to get them through the next month (if that). I often ask them what they plan to do in retirement and without fail, the answer that they usually give is that they plan to move back to their home countries and live off government benefits. This is an extremely dangerous proposition for two reasons: government mismanagement and ineligibility. I will discuss both of them in turn and you could also read this article by Andrew Hallam, "Top Ten Tips for International School Teachers to Build a Solid Retirement" which briefly mentions the same things.

Government Mismanagement

Government schemes such as the Canada Pension Plan (CPP) and old age security (whatever names they go by in your home country) are massive bureaucracies and subject to serious mishandling of funds. It is not so uncommon as to see scary line charts of promised payouts, which keep increasing into infinity and then another line, significantly below that with the payouts that are actually funded. The USA in particular seems to borrow from the present contributions to fund the daily operations of the government with little regard for the future. Basically, they are borrowing from future generations to over-spend in the present. Needless to say, any of these programs could see significant rollbacks by the time you or I reach retirement age in several ways: by reducing the amount of money received; not adjusting payouts for inflation; increasing the age at which these benefits are received; or cutting the program altogether. My advice is always to plan your retirement like you will receive *nothing* from the government in the way of benefits, and if you do, just think of it as "fun money" to live a bit more lavishly than you would otherwise be able to.

Ineligibility

The second reason is more particular to English teachers abroad. Things like the Canada Pension Plan require user contributions. If you are not working in your home country, you will not be accumulating funds and **will likely receive nothing in retirement.** Contrast this to someone who has lived in Canada their whole life: they would have been contributing a certain portion of their salary to the pension plan (it is mandatory and taken out of pay automatically), and even someone with a low-wage job would have accumulated a decent amount of money in the plan so that by the time they reach retirement, they will receive a basic amount each month, which they could in theory live on.

The other things to consider are health care and old age security payouts. You will have to check the details for yourself, but most countries have eligibility requirements based on the number of years lived in country during a certain period of time. If you have taught abroad for thirty-five of your forty working years, it is quite possible that you will not be eligible for these old age payouts or free health care programs. But, of course since it varies so much from country to country you need to check for yourself online and also consider your individual circumstances.

Step 7: Invest in the Financial Markets and Enjoy Life

Up until to this point, you have been working hard to pay off your debts and have been eating beans and rice, rice and beans. You have hopefully paid off all your debts, including student loans, built up a full emergency fund, and saved $5,000 to make your first investments. You have chosen a discount brokerage and transferred your first $5,000 to invest. During this period, I also hope you have been busy doing extensive research about investing, since it is an extremely valuable life skill which everyone should learn. Now, it is time to learn the practicalities about how to invest your money and enjoy life a bit more-- perhaps go on a vacation or buy something to reward yourself for all your hard work.

How to Buy a Stock or ETF

While this process varies a bit from brokerage to brokerage, the basic process is the same. All brokerages will also have a step by step tutorial or "help" section which explains the ins and outs of their own specific trading platform. **I highly recommend you take advantage of these resources**. You could also search on *YouTube* and you will likely find an unofficial tutorial for your chosen brokerage. For some brokerages, the mobile application that you can download to your phone (search for the company name in the App store and you will be able to find it) can sometimes be much easier to use than the website trading platform, so be sure to check that out as well. I use the mobile application for *Interactive Brokers* almost exclusively.

The first thing you need to do is transfer money from your bank account wherever you are working to your brokerage account. There are lots of options if you have an account in your home country and are transferring money from there, but if you are working overseas, there are usually few options but to do a wire transfer. It will cost you between ten and thirty dollars on both ends, but it is simple to do and any bank teller at any bank around the world should be able to initiate this. I do not recommend transferring money to your home country bank account first, and then to your brokerage, because you will end up paying more fees and possibly losing money on currency exchange twice instead of once. After you transfer money and it is accessible in your brokerage account, you will receive a confirmation of some kind, usually by email.

Once you get confirmation, it is time to make your trades. The process is the same for both ETFs and individual stocks. There are two basic trading options that you need to know: **market orders** and **limit orders**. If you put in a *market order*, you will be buying the stock or ETF at whatever price it is listed at on the market at that moment (during trading hours) or when the market opens the next day (for orders after trading hours). You can easily find the trading hours by going to the exchange's website, or your brokerage's website will often let you know you as well. If you use a *limit order*, your order will only be completed if the stock or ETF reaches the price that you have set, either higher than the market price if selling, or lower than the market price if buying. There are advantages and disadvantages to both of these trading options. A market order will always be completed, while a limit order may not; a market order is at the mercy of large swings in price but you will always complete the trade. For another explanation be sure to read, "What's the Difference Between a Market Order and a Limit Order?" on *Investopedia*.

It is rare for stock prices to have very large fluctuations, but it can happen, which I why *I recommend using limit orders.* Suppose you have put in a market order to sell a certain stock after trading hours (which is most often the case if you are living in Asia and trading on the North American markets). Overnight, some terrible fate befalls that company (like an oil spill) and when the markets open in the morning, the stock price is much lower than you expected it to be. Or perhaps your company has somehow had some extremely beneficial thing happen to them overnight (like a lucrative offer to buy the company) and you had a market order to buy. In the morning, the stock price is significantly higher than you expected it to be. However, these cases are rare, especially for ETFs (which are composed of hundreds of companies and news from one or two of these companies will not have a significant impact), or blue chip dividend paying stocks, which are mature companies whose stock price does not fluctuate so much, so you would probably be fine if you stuck with market orders, although I myself only use limit orders.

For a market order, you need to go to the brokerage's trading platform and enter the symbol for the stock or ETF that you want to buy. Then, select "market order," "buy," and enter the number of shares that you wish to buy. To sell, it is the same process except you choose "sell" instead of "buy." Remember that in the previous section, I recommended buying around $2,500 worth of each stock or ETF, so if stock ABC's share price is $100, you would want to buy 25 shares. However, if the stock price is $99.54, I would still buy 25 shares and not worry about being too exact. It does not matter that much and you just need to approximate.

A limit order is a bit more complicated but still reasonably easy. Enter the symbol of the stock or ETF, select "buy," "limit order," "GTC" (good until cancelled, or you can select a single day or period of time), number of shares and the price you want to buy at. For example, shares of stock XYZ are selling at $100 per share, but I want to get them for a little bit cheaper, I could put in a buy limit order on them for $99/share. If the stock goes down to $99, the order will be completed. However, if the stock does not go down to $99/share, the order will not be completed.

If you are selling, the principle is the same, except you will set a price higher than the current price. For example, stock XYZ has a market price of $100. I want to get a bit more money on the sale, so I set a sell limit order of $101. If the stock goes up to $101, the transaction will be completed but if it does not, the trade will not go through.

Before your make your first trades, here are my top 5 tips to avoid mistakes:

Top 5 Tips to Avoid Mistakes

Research Do NOT begin trading before you have done extensive research about investing. This book is just the beginning and I do not recommend making trades based on the information I give here alone.

Trading Tutorials Watch your company's tutorial on how to use their trading platform. You can probably find this in the "help" section of their website, or on *YouTube*.

Get Help Find an experienced friend or family member to help you, if possible. Do not ask for their advice about which stocks or ETFs to buy, but enlist their help for simply executing the trades.

Go Slowly If you watch the news and read the headlines, you can get the impression that everything is happening really quickly and that you need to take urgent action in response to the headlines. This is *never the case* and you should *always take your time* when making any investment decisions and in executing your trades.

Just do it! Most people never feel prepared enough to actually make their first trades, but at some point you just have to go for it. Start small, learn from your mistakes and keep honing your investment skills.

What Next? Collect Dividends and Keep Investing

Good news! Now that you have invested your first $5,000, you will collect some dividends in a few months. You actually do not have to do anything because the brokerage will automatically take off whatever withholding taxes they need to (it varies from country to country, depending on the exchange you bought on) and then automatically deposit the money into your account. Some brokerages offer a very small interest rate on that cash, but it is so low that it is not even worth considering leaving your money there for the long term. Remember that you are actually losing money on this due to inflation. Instead, keep transferring money from your day job into your brokerage account (tip: wire transfer fees can be expensive, so only do it when you have a least a couple thousand dollars, or more), which will be combined with these dividend payments.

Once you accumulate $2,500, you have two options. The first one is to choose another stock to buy. If you are investing in individual stocks, I recommend having around 20-25 of them in your portfolio because that provides a good level of diversification which reduces risk, but it is not too difficult to keep track of all those companies. The second option happens once you already have this allotted number of stocks (20-25) in your portfolio. At that point, with each additional $2,500 unit that you have either through dividend payments or your day job, buy some more stocks of one of your previous positions to bring it up to $5,000, instead of about $2,500. Similar to ETFs, you should choose whichever stock has the lowest cash value (at, or below $2,500) because that means that it is relatively cheap compared to the other stocks in your portfolio (which are hopefully higher than $2,500), as long as you are still happy owning that company's stock, and the sagging share price does not reflect a long-term weakness in the company.

Some brokerages (but often not the discount ones) offer a **dividend reinvestment plan (DRIP)**, where your dividend payments can be automatically set to go towards purchasing more shares (full or more commonly *fractional shares*) of the same stock. A **fractional share** is less than a single full share. For example, if a stock has a price of $100 and you get a dividend payment of $33, your DRIP plan would automatically buy approximately 1/3 of a full share. These plans are not terrible but I do not use them for a couple reasons. The first is that you can end up with a bunch of fractional shares which can be impossible to sell. Secondly, the stocks you are buying automatically may not actually be the ones you want to be buying for various reasons: your portfolio is already over-weighted with this stock, the company has recently cut their dividend (or has some other problem) and you are planning to sell it soon, or it is "expensive."

When to Sell a Stock or ETF

This is a simpler question to answer for ETFs than it is for stocks. For an ETF, the only time that you might sell is if you are rebalancing your portfolio. But, as mentioned in the section about ETFs, it is better to rebalance your portfolio through adding additional funds than it is by selling for the simple reason that it will reduce your trading costs; it does not actually matter if you rebalance exactly because it is the general principle that is most important. Another reason to sell an ETF would be if you are getting older and would like to increase the portion of your portfolio that you hold in bonds. But again, this is often possible to do just by adding additional funds to your brokerage account and buying only bond ETFs instead of stock ETFs as you get close to retirement. Always try to reduce your trading costs as much as possible and the best way to do this is by avoiding selling if at all possible.

In retirement, the goal is to live off dividend payments and other income streams that you develop and hopefully never have to touch the actual stocks or ETFs that generate those payments. However, you might find yourself in a situation where you do not generate enough income and have to sell some of your assets, which might be your ETFs. If I were retired and forced to sell an ETF, I would probably sell whatever generated the lowest interest rate/dividend payment, providing that it is "expensive" and did not recently have a significant price reduction in the past few months or years.

For stocks, the situation is a bit more complicated when deciding to sell or not. ETFs are diversified baskets of stocks, which means that while a single company's fortunes can have an impact upon the ETF as a whole, it usually has only a small influence. For example, *VT* has over 7,000 companies from around the world in it so one company having an oil spill or someone's servers getting hacked does not really matter that much. If you own individual stocks, it is an entirely different picture and so you need to be ready to sell, if necessary. The reasons that I would consider selling one of my dividend paying stocks are:

Dividend Cut I choose the stocks that I do based on their history of increasing dividends. If a company cuts the dividend, it is usually a sign of significant weakness and I would sell the stock, perhaps even taking a loss on share price in the process. However, if there is a good reason for the cut and the company's fundamentals (profits and competitive advantage are most important) remain strong, I would hold on and see what the next two or three years bring. A good reason for a dividend cut would include paying off relatively high-interest loans, an acquisition of another company, share buybacks to counteract a sagging stock price, or an emergency such as an oil spill where future payouts are unknown. If a company does not raise dividends for a year or two, it is less serious than a cut and I do not worry about it, but it will be on "watch closely status."

Change in Competitive Advantage I buy companies that are the leaders in their industries. For example, Apple is clearly a world leader in high-end consumer electronics and they generate huge amounts of cash, of which they are paying out increasing amounts as dividends to their shareholders. If a new upstart company started to gain more and more market share away from Apple, and Apple did nothing to counteract this, I would consider selling. You do not want to stick with a dying company, no matter how high the dividend is because the share price will keep going down and down as earnings fall (remember the price-earnings ratio, which generally finds its equilibrium at around fifteen over the very long term). As earnings go down, the company will eventually have to cut the dividend. Kodak is one such example of a company that was once an industry leader, but did not adapt to changing times.

Payout Ratio Closely related to earnings is the payout ratio. Remember that the payout ratio is the dividend payment in relation to net income. The lower the percentage the better, and I will never buy a stock with a ratio above 50%. If a company's payout ratio edges up into the 60's, I would keep an eye on it but not necessarily sell. Maybe the company just had a bad year with a reduction in income for some reason but will bounce back. When it gets into the 70's or higher, it is a sign of serious danger and I would probably sell.

You Need the Cash While it is preferable to keep dividend paying stocks forever (like ETFs), just living off of the income generated by them, it is possible that you might have to sell them to have additional retirement funds, or for something like a down payment on a house. Sell if you must, but whatever you do, DO NOT SELL LOW. The absolute worst time to sell is when the stock market crashes; remember that you need to manage your emotions and not be fearful. What goes down will probably come up again (unless it is a dying company!). I would sell whatever stock was "expensive," as indicated in the section, "Key Metrics I Look At."

Investing on the Margin

Companies often use debt to fund growth and individuals can do the same by using the **margin**, which is when your brokerage lends you money to invest, while charging you interest. However, this is not something that beginners should do and even advanced investors should proceed with caution. Brokerages offer varying margin rates and a company like Interactive Brokers, while offering a zero interest rate on deposits, has an almost similarly low rate for borrowing money. This rate is something you should consider when choosing a brokerage if you plan to use the margin.

People get into trouble when using the margin because they simply have too much debt. While the stock prices are up, the capital requirements (the amount of equity you have in your brokerage account) may be met, but if the market suddenly crashes, you may not have enough assets in the account to support the amount of debt you have (margin requirements vary from broker to broker so you need to *read the fine print carefully*) and your brokerage may automatically start selling your stocks at absolutely the worst time. Some may give you a courtesy call or email to give you a chance to choose which stocks or ETFs to sell, or add additional funds, but they do not have to by law.

Despite these dangers, it can be quite a good way to make money (but only for the advanced investor!!!). For example, Interactive Brokers currently has a margin rate of 1.63% for the first $100,000, while McDonalds (MCD) is paying a dividend of 3.70%. Even accounting for taxes on dividends (about 15%), there is a difference of 1.76% (3.70-1.63 x 0.85 = 1.76). Even better is an ETF like JNK that I hold in my own portfolio which yields 5.9% and would give you a final yield of 3.6% after interest and taxes. In essence, it is like "free-money," but again, proceed with caution. While my brokerage would actually give me far more money, my personal ratio is around 15-20%, which means that for every $100,000 I have invested, I borrow $15,000-$20,000 more on the margin. Even with a significant market crash like the one in 2008, I will not be forced to sell. Check out the article, "Buying Stock on the Margin 101," at *About Money* for another explanation of the pros and cons of using this method.

Speculative Stocks and ETFs

Friends often ask me about things like **marijuana stocks** or **TESLA**, **penny stocks** (stocks with a share price of less than a dollar), **IPO's** (initial public offerings--the first time it is possible to buy shares of a company on the open markets), **inverse ETFs** (acts in an opposite way--stock prices go up but this ETF will go down in value) and **micro-niche ETFs** (they cover very tiny slices of the market). These things are all bad for the beginner and I strongly recommend against them and suggest that people instead stick with blue chip dividend paying stocks (nothing wrong with investing like a grandma or grandpa) or ETFs that cover a broad slice of the market (like VT, VWO or BND).

Since marijuana became legal in some American states and TESLA started producing trendy cars, they are the cool new things that everyone wants to get a piece of, but they are largely unproven. There are no big, publicly traded companies (on the major exchanges like the New York Stock Exchange) in the marijuana industry as far as I know and probably will not be for another ten years or more. Who knows how TESLA will fare in the next ten or twenty years because they have serious competition from the world's major car-makers who are increasingly becoming interested in more environmentally friendly cars.

Penny stocks are stocks which are very cheap and under $1. They do not trade on the major exchanges and even if you can find a place to buy them, you are probably just throwing away your money. Most of these companies fail and you should invest your money, instead of gambling, which is what buying penny stocks actually is. You probably have a better chance at making money at the casino than you do "investing" in penny stocks!

IPOs or initial public offerings get a lot of hype. Remember when *Facebook* and *Twitter* went public and people could buy their stocks for the first time? Everyone wanted a piece of the action. The big problem is these stocks often are seriously overvalued due to the all the hype and you will end up paying way too much money for a company that might not even be generating a profit, as is the case for many of the trendy new technology companies. Why not wait a year or two and see what the situation looks like then? It is most often true that the *later* share price is cheaper than when it first went public. Or perhaps the company has still not figured out a way to make some profits, in which case you would not want to be a shareholder of that company. See "IPO Basics Tutorial," over at *Investopedia* for further details.

Inverse ETFs are designed to profit from a decline in a certain benchmark such as the S&P 500. While they can be helpful in protecting your portfolio from a serious decline, they are also extremely complicated and I would not recommend them for the average or beginner investor. Micro-niche ETFs such as SKYY (Cloud computing index) or TAN (Solar ETF) cover an extremely small corner of the market and are vulnerable to rapid fluctuations as well as sometimes being difficult to sell since there may be nobody willing to buy the shares that you are trying to sell.

Futures Contracts, and Shorting Stocks

I remember about ten years ago, when I was researching about investing, I had a conversation with a good English teacher friend about how he was investing his money. I use the term investing quite loosely here because he was actually buying up **futures contracts** on the commodities markets (you can find details about this strategy on *Investopedia)*. He started diagraming it out for me and it became more and more complicated, so that I actually had no idea what he was talking about. By that time, I had done extensive research into investing, so I was no newbie, but it was like he was speaking some sort of foreign language. I shared my own plan to invest for the long-term in blue chip dividend paying stocks and he kind of scoffed at me and wondered why I would do that when I was still in my twenties. I took his joking good-naturedly and said, "Let's see how we're each doing ten years from now." We are still friends and as far as I know, my net worth is far, far greater than his. As it turned out, my 'boring' style worked out pretty well for me, as it will for you too.

Futures contracts and things like *shorting stocks* are complicated and <u>not for the average investor</u>. When you **short a stock**, you try to profit as the stock price goes down but it comes with considerable risk if the stock price actually goes up instead of down. For more details, check out this helpful article on *Investopedia.* I consider myself an advanced investor but I still would not consider using these instruments. Becoming proficient at buying ETFs and dividend paying stocks, rebalancing your portfolio, avoiding excessive taxes, and planning your retirement years carefully is enough of a challenge without adding all these other complications and risks.

Enjoy Life a Bit

Life is looking pretty good right now, isn't it? You have your emergency fund so you are not worried about a medical emergency or a pet getting sick. You are knowledgeable about the stock market, have confidently invested your money and are collecting dividend payments, and there are no more debts hanging over your head causing you to lose sleep. While you should still be living on a budget, you can take your foot off the brakes and ease up a bit. Save for a vacation, or a toy like a new computer.

Now that you are out of debt, you should never go back into it, with the exception of buying a house so do not even consider putting these things on your credit card. Instead, open another bank account, preferably a high-interest one and call it your "fun money" account. I recommend using the 70-20-10 rule (or whatever ratio you want it to be). If you save $1000 per month, you would put $700 towards investing, $200 towards long-term fun (which would go in that separate "fun money" bank account), and use $100 for short-term fun. The long-term fun money account could be used to save for something like a new computer, vacation, or car, while the short-term fun money can be used to expand your monthly budget and do stuff like eat out, see a movie or buy an expensive bottle of wine. You have been working hard! Enjoy it.

The Cost per Use Model

Now that you have paid off your debts and invested some money, you are perhaps saving money and contemplating purchasing a toy of some sort with your "long-term fun money" account. A helpful way to look at a bigger purchase is the **cost per use** model. For example, I recently bought a stand up paddleboard for about $600, which is quite expensive in my world. However, I had used this item numerous times before while I was on vacation, knew that I was addicted, and also that I would use it a lot. Here are my estimates:

Cost: $600

Usage: 2-3 times a week, 6 months of the year

Total usage: 60 times/year

Cost per use, first year: $10/use

Cost per use, after 2 years: $5/use (based on 120 total uses)

Considering that the cost for a rental is around $40 here in Korea, the cost per use in the first year of only $10 is extremely cheap. I also hope to be able to sell the board for $200-300 when I leave Korea, which further reduces my cost per use. If I had only used the board three times per year, for two years, my cost per use would have been $100, which obviously would not have been a good purchase for me. However, at $5 per use after two years, it is a very good deal and an excellent frugal hobby, despite the initial high cost.

Another way to think about cost per use is **cost per <u>hour</u>**. Recently my friends bought a nice flat screen TV and had it installed on the wall. The total cost for the TV and installation was around $500. I asked my friends how much TV they watch and they laughed and said way too much, probably around twenty hours per week for the two of them together. Here are my estimates for their situation:

Cost: $500

Total usage/week: 20 hours

Total usage/year: 1,040 hours

Cost per use, first year: $0.48/hour

Cost per use, after 2 years: $0.24/hour (based on 2080 total hours of use)

Clearly, this is an extremely cheap hobby for my friends because what else could they do that costs so little, but which they are happy to do for such large amounts of time each week. If they only watched TV for one hour per week, clearly this purchase would have been a poor choice for them because the cost per hour used would have been very high.

Budget Travel Tips

Most people go abroad to teach because they want to travel and see the world, eat new food and experience different cultures, languages and people. The first thing that most of us English teachers want to do when we get a bit of vacation time is take an exotic vacation somewhere out of the country we are teaching in. After you have paid off your debts, filled your emergency fund and begun to invest in the stock market, it really is possible to do this (guilt free). I have been to over thirty countries during my ten years abroad and have done all my trips quite cheaply. Here are my top tips for budget travel:

Be flexible I usually know that I want to go somewhere on vacation, but I never really have a specific place in mind, or a specific time period (I get almost twenty weeks of vacation at my job so can go anytime really). I will open up a few tabs on my browser and go to the discount carriers such as Air Asia and Cebu Pacific and see what kind of deals I can find from my city to a few different destinations, using the search over a period of time instead of specific days function. When I find something cheap to a place I want to go to, I book it.

Stay with Friends or Family When I went to graduate school in Vancouver, Canada, there were many international students and lots of them were from Europe. During my time in Korea, I also met many people from England who have returned home for work or school. When I wanted to go to Europe, the obvious choice was to contact all these old friends and mention that I was coming. Without fail, all of them offered me a place to stay and generously even organized for me to stay at their friend or parent's houses in different cities. I ended up traveling around Germany, France, England, the Netherlands and Belgium for almost ten weeks and only had to stay in a hotel for four nights during that period. Many of my meals were covered as well as people usually insisted on cooking for me, or taking me out (of course I returned the favor by buying a few groceries and cooking for them or buying a few drinks out). In the end, I spent far less money than I would have ever thought possible in Europe and came home with a few hundred Euros still in my pocket. If you do not have friends or family members in interesting places, check out *Couch Surfing*, which is where you can stay with people for free.

Volunteer Another way to stay cheaply for a long time in a place is to volunteer. While you often have to pay your own way there, you can sometimes find a place where you can get free accommodation and/or food and drinks. One winter vacation, I volunteered at a cooking school/bar/restaurant/bungalow in Koh Lanta, Thailand for ten weeks, with all the profits supporting an animal shelter on the island. In return for working at the reception desk for forty hours per week, I got free accommodation and food, as well as half price (and many free thanks to the owner and generous tourists who found out I was a volunteer) drinks at the bar, along with meeting plenty of amazing people. It ended up being another extremely cheap vacation and I spent far less than I thought I would have (as an aside, check out the fabulous *Time for Lime* for yourself).

Do Not Book Ahead When I travel somewhere, I will generally book the first couple nights in a hostel or hotel after I get off the plane because it is quite dangerous to be wandering around in the dark, alone in a new city and looking for a place to stay. After that, it really is much cheaper to find something once you have your boots on the ground because the cheapest stuff is often not advertised on sites like *Agoda.* This is especially true if you will be arriving in a new place during daylight hours. The same applies for any sort of tours or transportation, which are always a rip-off when booked online from abroad instead of on the ground at your destination.

Choose Only a Few Places The most expensive way to travel is to always be on the road because you never learn where the best places to eat are, or where the cheapest laundry place is, or where the half price happy hour can be found. When you are always on the move, it can be extremely tiring and when you are in this state, it is so easy to make impulse purchases or break your budget with an expensive taxi ride simply because you are exhausted. Of course, the biggest expense that comes from moving around every couple of days is the transportation costs, which in some countries can end up being the biggest expense of the trip. I recommend staying in a place for at least four or five days to maximize your budget travel.

Food If your hostel or hotel offers "free" breakfast, make sure you take full advantage of it, especially if it is a delicious buffet. If this is the case, I will eat a lot for breakfast, a small snack for lunch and then a nice dinner later. You can save a lot of money this way. Otherwise, if breakfast is not included in your accommodation, get out of the habit of eating three full meals a day. Just go with street food or a quick snack from a bakery/convenience/grocery store for at least one of the meals, and preferably two. Street food, especially in South-East Asia is really delicious and reasonably healthy.

Step 8: Build Passive Income Streams

Now that you have made a wise decision about your career, paid off your debts, built a full emergency fund, and have begun to invest in the stock market, it is time to turn to alternative sources of income besides teaching. In order to build wealth, it is essential to recognize that you do not need to do an hour of labor to get paid for an hour. You do this at your day job teaching English where you sign a contract to teach a certain number of hours for a certain amount of pay, which is fine but it can be very helpful to have other income streams working for you, preferably passive ones. By **passive income streams**, I mean that you have to put time and effort into getting them set up ONE TIME but after you do it, they require minimal maintenance and time. The good news is that you already have one passive income stream because you have invested money in the stock market and you now collect the dividends each month.

Some other passive income streams that have been useful to me are: HubPages, *Amazon Associates, Iherb, Agoda* and writing a book using *Amazon* as my platform. I will talk about them in turn, giving some useful tips but remember that there are many, many more opportunities for building passive income streams and you should find whatever works for you.

HubPages

My first foray into the world of passive income stream building, apart from dividend stocks was with *Squidoo* (which later merged with *HubPages*) about five years ago on the recommendation of a friend. Initially, results were not that promising and I was only earning $10-20 per month but I still remember the excitement when I made my first sale: a *Lonely Planet Korea* guidebook on a site about places to visit in South Korea. As time went by, I built more and more pages and started to generate a significant amount of income, always more than $100 per month. I have not put any real effort into *HubPages* in the last three years, but I still earn a decent amount of money ($60-90 per month) and during the past five years, I have earned around $5,000 which I have used to fund my exotic vacations around the world. It is passive income at its best!

You earn income from *HubPages* in two basic ways: selling products on *Amazon* or *Ebay*, for which you get a commission of 4-10%, depending on a number of factors, or by getting a share of the advertising revenue, your proportion of which is calculated by page views. If you have a really popular site with plenty of views, you can get quite a high proportion of ad money. Or, if you sell lots of products, you can also generate significant income that way. The best possible scenario is a site that gets a lot of traffic and also makes a lot of sales of high end products. I have one *HubPage* reviewing ESL textbooks which makes a lot of sales, but only generates around $1/book sale in income. Conversely, my scuba diving camera site makes only one or two sales per month, but for some of the more expensive cameras, I can get more than $20 in commission.

The key to getting popular on *HubPages* is first by having quality content. It is best to write about things that you have some authority about so that people will trust what you have to say. If you want to write about something which you have no prior knowledge about, extensive research will be required. It is ideal if you write about things that have lots of *Google* searches, but low competition from other websites. You can do a bit of keyword research on *Google Adwords* (keywords) to find this. It is beyond the scope of this book but there are a lot of podcasts, websites and books about SEO (search engine optimization) that you could check out if you are interested.

Affiliate Programs

When you sign up for an **affiliate program**, you advertise a company's products in return for a commission, which varies from company to company. You will often need to have a professional looking blog or website with a decent amount of traffic in order for a company to accept you into their program. Remember, it is *always* better to sell things on your websites which you use or like. It is more authentic and you will be able to sleep at night, feeling like you helped people instead of convincing people to buy useless junk. The best thing about affiliate programs is that you can earn money selling things without worrying about the hassle of having to sell the actual product yourself. The company you are advertising for takes care of all that. Most affiliate programs either pay you via *Paypal* or with credit for orders from the company itself. I will discuss some of my favorite affiliate programs for teachers abroad.

Amazon

Amazon is the first affiliate program anyone with a website should sign up for. As I am sure you already know, Amazon sells everything and I mean this quite literally. It is easy to join their program and depending on the payment structure you choose, you can make between four and ten percent commission on any product you sell. The good news is that it is not only the specific product that you have advertised, but it is any purchase made by someone who has clicked any of your links. There are two basic ways to earn a lot of money: by selling big ticket items or by making lots of sales.

The best way to make money on Amazon is by giving people valuable information through a blog post of some kind and then recommending a related product of some kind that either solves a problem which people might have or gives further information. For example, I have a website giving information about which kind of scuba diving fins to buy and then I have various Amazon links for the different kinds of fins. An example of additional information would be my various financial websites where I give information about investing strategies and then recommend some books that offer more in-depth information than I have listed on the site.

Iherb

Another affiliate program which expats should consider is Iherb. I know it is a strange name, but they are a totally legitimate company which sells health food and supplements. Iherb is especially fabulous for the vegetarian or picky eater who lives overseas; you really should just take a look at their website for yourself. The way their affiliate program works is that you share your personal code or personalized link wherever you want. You do not need to have a website, but you could share it on Facebook, by email or anywhere else you can think of. You are automatically signed up for their program with your first order. The person who uses your code or link gets $5-10 off their first order, depending on size and you get around 4% in commission for the first year on any of their orders. This amount gets lower in subsequent years and you also earn a smaller commission on orders if the person you referred refers other people. The amount of money you need to have pooled (accumulated commission on multiple purchases by multiple people) in order to get a cash payout is $300, but you can use lower amounts in credit towards your purchases, which is what I usually do since I love *Iherb's* products and I put in an order a few times a year.

A couple of *Iherb* strategies that have worked for me are to point out shipping deals and have lots of friends! The latter one involves spending time with expats and mentioning Iherb whenever someone says, "I miss XYZ from home" or, "I wonder where I can XYZ?" The answer I almost always give is *Iherb* and then I mention that they can get some money off on their first order if they use my link, which I send to them as soon as possible. The other strategy is to pay attention to shipping deals, which seem to happen almost monthly, at least to South Korea. Shipping to Korea is already pretty cheap at four dollars or so, but there is often free shipping, and I will be sure to post it as my *Facebook* status and perhaps in a few *Facebook* groups I am in which I know are likely to have people interested in it.

Agoda

Whenever I travel and have to use an Internet site to book hotels, I will always use *Agoda*. They have many hotel choices, including budget ones, helpful reviews from other customers and a generous loyalty program. I looked into their referral program at one point and was astounded to find out that they offer commissions of up to 60%. Sadly, my websites are not directly related to travel and I got rejected from their program. However, if you have a travel website, *Agoda* could be a very profitable option for you to consider.

Writing E-books

I wrote my first e-book, "*How to Get an English Teaching Job in South Korea: The English Teaching Job of Your Dreams*" because on my blog, "*My Life! Teaching in a Korean University*," the majority of the questions I got were related to getting a job teaching in a Korean university. I have taught in Korean universities for about ten years and as a result, I have a lot of knowledge about this topic but upon searching the Internet for information related to this, I realized that there was almost none. It was an ideal situation because I could give information that many people wanted, but for which there was essentially no real competition. Similar to this book, I find that many of my English teaching friends have lots of questions about personal finance and more specifically investing and while there is a wealth of information out there, none of it is specific to ESL/EFL teachers overseas.

Writing the book itself was not that difficult since I had already covered many of the topics on my blog and on other websites such as *HubPages*. The part that I was most intimidated about was the actual formatting and publishing of the book. My fear, however was misplaced as it was much easier than I expected and if you use *Amazon*, they have plenty of helpful tutorials about how to do it correctly.

Top 5 Tips for Self-Publishing an E-Book

Here are my top five tips to help get you started with self-publishing your first book. **First**, consider your topic carefully. It is a lot of work to publish a book and you will want to make it worth your time. By considering your topic carefully, I mean that you should try to find something that has very little competition and on which you are an authority.

Second, do not underestimate the editing process. I recommend getting a friend who majored in English language and literature, or who has a background in editing to do it for you; I posted on Facebook as my status update that I was looking for an editor and I had several friends offer to help me. Of course you should offer to write your friend a recommendation letter or act as a reference of some kind if required.

Third, go with *Amazon* at first. It is the leading website/self-publishing platform in the world and the website that will be most likely to come up first on *Google* or *Yahoo*. Even more importantly, *Amazon* is the site that people trust and buy from. In addition, you can use *Amazon's Create Space* to easily make a physical, print on demand copy of your book.

Fourth, try to limit the amount of paid advertising that you use. Ideally, you will already have sites set up related to the topic such as a blog or various *HubPages*. Another way to advertise for free is to contact people in your field who have blogs and ask them to review your book. I send these people a *free* copy and offer to write some guest posts. It also helps if you have a well-respected website of some sort so that you can offer to feature their site on it.

Finally, do not give up. It is easy to get bogged down trying to figure out the formatting thing if you are not especially good at computer stuff (me!), designing a cover if you are not that creative or good at graphic design (me!), or get frustrated when your editor comes back with more changes than you ever thought would be possible (thank you Jason). Persevere until the end of the process because it will be worth it when you are earning passive income.

If you are really interested in self-publishing your own books, a few podcasts that I find helpful are: *The Publishing Profits Podcast Show*, *Self Publishing Questions,* and *Self Publishing Answers.* They are all very easy to find just by searching on *iTunes*.

Step 9: Plan for the Future--Working and Insurance

Working

Let me start with a little story about myself. During my first few years working at Korean universities, I had plenty of free time since I only worked around twenty hours per week and I had three to four months of vacation per year. What did I do with that time? Nothing really of substance, I am kind of ashamed to admit. I took exotic vacations all over the world (which I am happy about), but I also did many things I regret such as watching a lot of TV, hanging out with people who were not really good for me and wasting money on too many restaurant meals and nights out. I truly wish I had used that time in a better way to either improve my professional skills as they relate to my career, or to develop passive income streams. So what I am ultimately saying is this: even though teaching overseas is a pretty easy job, *do not waste your time* and use the opportunity that you have to do something that will help you in the future. Some things that you could consider if you want to continue teaching abroad are an online master's program (TESOL, Education, English, or Linguistics are generally preferred) of some kind so that university jobs are open for you, or an English teaching certificate such as the CELTA or DELTA.

If you plan to return to your home country, perhaps you could get an online diploma in something very practical such as accounting so that it will be easy for you to find employment when you return. You could also get some certifications in whatever field you want to move into you after you finish teaching. Or, you could study for something like the LSAT and apply for schools when you are abroad. I have been in Korea for a decade and have seen plenty of people come and go. The ones that are most successful leaving and returning home are the ones who have a detailed plan for where they are going to live and what kind of job they are going to get. The ones who go home to live in their parent's basement and *just find a job* are the people who burn through their money in no time and are back teaching abroad in less than a year. By using your time abroad well, and planning and preparing for your return home you can be in the latter category and not the former.

Is Insurance Necessary?

Of course there are times when insurance is necessary like if you have a car, but other times it is a lot more ambiguous and really depends on individual circumstances. I will talk about two kinds of insurance (supplementary health insurance and life insurance) where it really depends on your individual circumstances whether you would need them or not.

Supplementary Health Insurance

For the sake of simplicity, I am going to assume that we are not talking about the USA, but about every single other developed country in the entire world that has some form of national health care. Of course these plans differ, but many of them do not cover things like prescription drugs, ambulance rides, or dental care. Here in Korea, it is partly user pay and partly government funded so that for something like cancer, you can actually end up paying a significant portion out of pocket, especially if you want to get treated at the top hospitals in the country. However, something like going to the doctor for a cold or the dentist for a check-up is basically free, including medication.

So is supplementary health insurance necessary? For me, the answer is no because I am young and very healthy. Also, the insurance I get through the Korean government covers a decent amount and if I were to get sick, my emergency fund of $10,000 US would hopefully cover the rest. If not, I would be able to get a lot more money through selling some of my investments, although it would take a bit of time. For anything serious, I get a significant discount at the hospital run by the university I work at, so I would have to pay less than other people. Finally, even though there is a three month waiting period, I could return to Canada and receive free health care for something that is serious, but not urgent. Basically, I am self-insured.

But what about for other people living and working overseas? The answer is probably yes if you do not have a full emergency fund (3-6 months of living expenses) and/or significant investments. The answer is also probably yes if you are unhealthy and/or older (50+). Lastly, it is also probably a yes if you have kids. If it is you, your spouse and 2 kids, the chance that someone will get sick or seriously injured is much greater than for just a single person.

Life Insurance

Life insurance is something that a lot of people ignore, to their own peril. That said, I have met many people over the years that have life insurance and I really have no idea why. The purpose of life insurance is to provide for *dependents* in case of death. **Dependents** is the key word here. If you do not have children or a spouse that requires your salary in order to live, then you really do not need life insurance. However, if you have children or a spouse that depend on your salary, you need life insurance. Even a stay at home spouse with young kids should have life insurance because if they were to die, childcare costs could be significant.

Of course, similar to supplementary health insurance is if you have a significant emergency fund of *one year's **salary** (or more), **significant** investments and no debt*, you probably do not need life insurance even if you have kids because you are essentially self-insured.

There are two kinds of life insurance to consider, whole life and term insurance. Of the two, term insurance is *by far* the better choice for various reasons which I will discuss. What exactly are these two products? Check out *Insurance Comparison's* definitions (although you should not jump to the conclusion that whole life insurance is better like they did):

"**Whole life insurance** is a continual policy that is paid throughout the entire life of the individual from the moment the payments begin. These premium payments will remain the same and they are often quite a bit higher in cost than a term life policy. This is the major downside of a whole life policy. These types of policies actually accrue interest overtime and people can use this money for emergencies if they need to.
A **term life insurance** policy is in effect for only a set period of time. The premiums are smaller initially, which is the main positive of this type. However, the premiums increase over time and they do not accrue interest in the manner of a whole life policy. The individual cannot regain money spent on this policy unless the policy holder dies"

If you listen to any of the financial gurus out there such as Dave Ramsey, Suze Orman, or Steve Peasley they all say the same thing: *avoid whole life insurance* and stick with term.

Here is a quote I like from *Wealth Pilgrim*:

> "The purpose of term life insurance is to protect your family for a specific time period. If you buy the right term life insurance, it does the job beautifully well. On the other hand, whole life insurance has two purposes. The first is to protect your family. The second . . . is to make insurance companies and agents lots of money. That's why *term life insurance is bought* while *whole life insurance is sold*."

My thoughts are that if you are going to invest, you should do extensive research and then buy ETFs that cover the broad market, or individual dividend paying stocks. If you are going to get life insurance, you should get the simplest thing possible that will protect your family and of course buy from a reputable company. Your life insurance policy is useless if the company goes bankrupt due to poor business practices. What you want is a term life insurance which covers you for a set amount of money for a certain period of time, for a certain fee which you pay. Combining your investments and your insurance into one product is way too confusing and it helps the insurance company a whole lot more than it helps you. You are far better off to buy term insurance, which is much cheaper than whole life and then take that extra money and invest it in the stock market yourself. Make your money work for you and not line the pockets of some insurance company representative.

Step 10: Enjoy Financial Freedom

Congratulations! Once you have made it to step ten, you will have paid off all your debts, fully-funded an emergency fund, invested a significant amount of money in either ETFs or dividend paying stocks, created some passive income streams and finally made a plan for your future career, whether that involves returning home or continuing to teach abroad. It is now time to enjoy your hard earned financial freedom. What exactly does this mean? If I had to boil it down to one word, it would be this: choices. You are no longer a slave to your job and if you are really unhappy, you can just quit. If you are living somewhere and no longer like it, you can just leave. If you decide that you do not want to teach anymore and want to go back to school and find a new career, you can. If your friends or family members are going on some amazing once-in-a-lifetime vacation, you can go too. If you want to volunteer for a few months for a cause that you think is worthwhile, you can. If you want to build a little cabin in the woods somewhere and live off the land, it is possible. If you want to buy that amazing new toy that you have had your eyes on for years, you should. Anything is possible (within reason!) when you are financially free. Enjoy it!

Remember this simple maxim: if you want to achieve financial freedom, you need to spend less than you earn and avoid debt, consistently, for the rest of your life. Take this extra money and deploy it wisely through investing and you will likely be rich by the time you retire. It really is that easy. Now, go do it!

Before You Go...

A few quick reminders before you go (keep reading for information about taxes, and links to my favorite resources). Email me (jb.business.online@gmail.com) with any questions or comments that you have. I would love to help you in any way that I can on your journey towards securing your financial future.

If you enjoyed the book and found it useful, please head over to Amazon and leave a review. It will help other teachers, like yourself get started on the journey towards financial freedom.

You may also be interested in some of these other books that I've written (you can find them easily on Amazon):

109 Personal Finance Tips: Things you Should Have Learned in High School.

49 ESL Conversation Games and Activities for Teenagers and Adults.

101 Activities and Resources for Teaching English Online.

Resources: Tax Information for Expats

It is with some trepidation that I write this since I am not an international tax expert, nor am I an accountant. I, myself, consult an international tax accountant for anything besides the most basic of questions that I can find answers to on the Internet. However, after many hours searching around on the Internet, I can say with certainty that I have found some excellent sites for you to _do your own research,_ which will certainly be better than the (mis)information that gets spread around the expat bars and online gossip forums with alarming regularity. The best case scenario is that you would have consulted an international tax accountant before you left your home country. The next best option is to spend a few hours doing your own research on the Internet for advice specific to your own country. Here are a few places for you to get started.

Canadians

Canadians are required to pay Canadian taxes on their international income if they are considered a resident of Canada for that taxation year. The good news is that the tax you pay in the other country gets deducted from your tax bill, provided that Canada and that country have a tax treaty of some sort. There are a number of factors that determine whether or not you are considered a resident of Canada but they have to do with primary and secondary ties, primary ones being something like a house or dependent children and secondary ones being things like membership in professional organizations, health coverage or bank accounts. It is in your best interests to cut as many of these ties as possible in order to ensure you are not considered a resident of Canada during your time abroad. If you leave Canada for only a year or two, do not bother with this, because you will almost always have to pay Canadian taxes on your international income; there is just no way around it. Most of the information I found said that upon leaving Canada, file one final tax return stating that you are leaving Canada on the first page and then do not file again until you return to Canada.

There is some debate about whether or not you should file the form NR-73, which is a _non-binding_ opinion from the Canadian Revenue Agency about whether or not they would consider you a resident, or not. It seems that most expat "accountants" you meet in the bar say you should, but that most international tax accountants recommend against it. You should make your own decision on this one and I am not going to give you any advice one way or the other.

A quick note about RRSPs (registered retirement savings plans) and TFSAs (tax free savings accounts): Canadian expats are not eligible to invest in them. You might also consider selling them before you leave Canada in order to reduce your secondary ties, but again, consult an *international* tax accountant for the best advice.

Proviso: Let me repeat that I am not an expert or authority on taxes and you should do your own research or consult a professional to make sure the information I have given in this book or in the links below is accurate.

Canadian Tax Treaties

(http://www.fin.gc.ca/treaties-conventions/in_force--eng.asp)

Determining your Residency Status

(http://www.cra-arc.gc.ca/tx/nnrsdnts/cmmn/rsdncy-eng.html)

Simplified Information from the Canadian Government's Travel Office

(http://travel.gc.ca/travelling/living-abroad/taxation)

Individuals Leaving or Entering Canada and Non-Residents

(http://www.cra-arc.gc.ca/tx/nnrsdnts/ndvdls/menu-eng.html)

Should You File NR-73?

(http://thecanadianexpat.com/index.php/members-only/resources/articles/taxes-a-finances/125-tax-implications-of-moving-to-the-middle-east)

Tax Basics for Canadian Expats

(http://www.expatica.com/nl/finance/tax/Tax-basics-for-Canadian-expats_101163.html)

Andrew Hallam-Investing for Canadian Expats

(http://andrewhallam.com/category/expat-investing/canadians-expat-investing/)

Americans

I have some good news for Americans because unlike Canadians, most teachers abroad will not have to pay American income taxes in addition to the taxes they pay in the country where they are teaching. This is because the US has a tax exemption for about the first $96,000 (it increases yearly) of income earned abroad, if you lived outside the US for 330 days out of the year. Even though you will likely not pay any taxes, it is required that you file a tax return every year.

One thing that you do need to be cautious about is contributing illegally to your IRA. You should really check out Andrew Hallam's *The Expatriate's Guide to Investing* and more specifically the section, "Investing for American Expats," but the gist of it is that you cannot invest in your IRA if you earn less than the tax exempt amount (around $96,000). If you do, it will count as *excess contributions* and you will face penalties. *Again, consult an international tax accountant for all the details and make sure to do your own research to ensure that the information given in these links is accurate and up to date.*

Tax Guide for U.S. Citizens and Resident Aliens Abroad

(http://www.irs.gov/publications/p54/)

Taxes for Americans Living Overseas

(http://www.reachtoteachrecruiting.com/us-taxes-for-english-teachers-abroad.html)

United States Income Tax Treaties

(http://www.irs.gov/Businesses/International-Businesses/United-States-Income-Tax-Treaties---A-to-Z)

American Expat Taxes

(https://www.expatriatetaxreturns.com/american-expat-taxes/)

Roth IRA Rules While Living Abroad

(http://rothiraaccountrules.com/roth-ira-rules-while-living-abroad/)

Andrew Hallam-Investing for American Expats

(http://andrewhallam.com/category/expat-investing/americans-expat-investing/)

Non North-Americans

Australia

Working Overseas

(https://www.ato.gov.au/Individuals/International-tax-for-individuals/Going-overseas/Working-overseas/)

Income Tax

(http://www.expatfocus.com/expatriate-australia-taxation)

Tax Advice for Expats

(http://www.exfin.com/tax-advice-expatriates)

Andrew Hallam-Investing for Australian Expats

(http://andrewhallam.com/category/expat-investing/australians-expat-investing/)

New Zealand

Tax Residency and Status

(http://www.ird.govt.nz/international/residency/)

Who Needs to File a Tax Return?

(http://www.ird.govt.nz/income-tax-individual/filing-your-return/overseas/)

Tax Treaties

(http://www.ird.govt.nz/international/residency/dta/?utm_source=newzealandnow.govt.nz)

Andrew Hallam-Investing for Kiwi Expats

(http://andrewhallam.com/category/expat-investing/new-zealand/)

The UK

Tax When Leaving the UK

(http://webarchive.nationalarchives.gov.uk/
+/http://www.hmrc.gov.uk/pensioners/taxwhenleaving.htm)

Tax Laws Clarified for Expatriates

(http://www.expatinfodesk.com/news/2011/09/17/uk-tax-laws-clarified-for-british-expatriates/)

Residency and Domicile

(http://britishexpats.com/articles/finance/uk-tax-residency-and-domicile/)

Andrew Hallam-Investing for British Expats

(http://andrewhallam.com/category/expat-investing/british-expat-investing/)

Resources: Books, Websites and Podcasts

Books

Bolen, Jackie. *How to Get a University Job in South Korea.*

Carrel, Lawrence. *Dividend Stocks for Dummies.*

Chilton, David. *The Wealthy Barber Returns. (www.wealthybarber.com)*

Graham, Benjamin. *The Intelligent Investor. (www.grahaminvestor.com)*

Hallam, Andrew. *The Global Expatriate's Guide to Investing/Millionaire Teacher.* (www.andrewhallam.com)

Lynch, Peter and John Rothchild. *One Up on Wall Street.*

Ramsey, Dave. *The Total Money Makeover.* (www.daveramsey.com)

Schultheis, Bill. *The New Coffee House Investor: How to Build Wealth, Ignore Wall Street and Get on With Your Life.*

Wild, Russell. *Exchange Traded Funds for Dummies/Index Investing for Dummies.*

Websites: Investing 101 for Beginners

About Money. "The Complete Beginner's Guide to Investing in Stock" *(http://beginnersinvest.about.com/od/stocktrading/tp/guide-to-investing-in-stocks.htm)*

Dividend Monk. "Dividend Stocks: The Essential Guide" (www.dividendmonk.com/dividend-stocks)

Investopedia. "6 Dangerous Moves for Beginner Investors" (www.investopedia.com/articles/basics/11/dangerous-moves-first-time-investors.asp)

Investopedia. "Stock Basics Tutorial" (www.investopedia.com/university/stocks)

The Simple Dollar. "The Five Most Important Factors in Your Investment Success" (www.thesimpledollar.com/five-most-important-factors-for-investment-success)

The Street. "How to Invest in Stocks" (http://www.thestreet.com/topic/47701/how-to-invest-in-stocks.html)

Vanguard. "ETF Investing Can Add Flexibility to your Portfolio"
(https://investor.vanguard.com/etf/)

Vanguard. "Vanguard's Principles for Investing Success"
(https://personal.vanguard.com/us/insights/investingtruths)

YouTube. "Stock Market For Dummies-A Beginner's Introduction to Stock Markets"
(www.youtube.com/watch?v=HYZgLVO6koQ)

Websites: Investing

Dividend Growth Investor (www.dividendgrowthinvestor.com)

Dividend Ninja (www.dividendninja.com)

Dividends Value (www.dividendsvalue.com)

Freedom Through Passive Income (www.freedomthroughpassiveincome.com)

Investopedia (www.investopedia.com)

"Stocks vs Bonds vs Gold-Past 200 Years"

(www.joshuakennon.com/stocks-vs-bonds-vs-gold-returns-for-the-past-200-years)

The Dividend Monk (www.dividendmonk.com)

The Simple Dollar (www.thesimpledollar.com)

Vanguard (www.vanguard.com)

Yahoo Finance (www.finance.yahoo.com)

Websites: Brokerages

DBS Vickers (www.dbsvickers.com)

Interactive Brokers (www.interactivebrokers.com)

Saxo Capital Markets (www.saxomarkets.com)

Schwab (www.schwab.com)

Sogotrade (www.sogotrade.com)

TD Direct Investing (www.tddirectinvesting.com)

Vanguard (www.vanguard.com)

Websites: Teaching Jobs

ESL Cafe (www.eslcafe.com)

Higher Ed Jobs (www.higheredjobs.com)

Profs Abroad (www.profsabroad.com)

TEFL Jobs Overseas (www.tefljobsoverseas.com)

TEFL Tips (www.tefl-tips.com)

TESOL International (www.tesol.org)

Vitae (www.chroniclevitae.com)

Websites: Passive Income

Amazon Create Space (www.createspace.com)

Amazon Affiliates (www.affiliate-program.amazon.com)

Amazon Kindle Direct Publishing (www.kdp.amazon.com)

Freedom Through Passive Income (www.freedomthroughpassiveincome.com)

Google Adwords (www.adwords.google.com)

HubPages (www.hubpages.com)

Iherb (www.iherb.com)

Smart Passive Income - Pat Flynn (www.smartpassiveincome.com)

Suitcase Entrepreneur - Natalie Sisson (www.suitcaseentrepreneur.com)

Wordpress - the site I recommend to blog at (www.wordpress.com)

Financial Calculators

Compound Interest Calculator
(www.moneychimp.com/calculator/compound_interest_calculator.htm)

Credit Card/Student Loan Payment Calculator
(https://www.creditkarma.com/calculators/debtrepayment)

Retirement Withdrawal Calculator (www.estimatepension.com/Retirement-Withdrawal-Calculator.aspx)

Podcasts: Investing

CNBC's The Suze Orman Show (www.suzeorman.com)

Dave Ramsey (www.daveramsey.com)

Invest Talk (www.investtalk.com)

Money Girl's Quick and Dirty Tips (www.quickanddirtytips.com/money-girl)

Motley Fool Money (www.fool.com)

Planet Money-NPR (www.npr.org/blogs/money)

The Money Tree Investing Podcast (www.moneytreepodcast.com)

Podcasts: Passive Income Building

Natalie Sisson's The Suitcase Entrepreneur (www.suitcaseentrepreneur.com)

The Freedom Lovin' Podcast (www.freedomlovin.com)

The Smart Passive Income Podcast (www.smartpassiveincome.com)

Manufactured by Amazon.ca
Acheson, AB

13562193R00055